MORE BULLETIN BOARD-ERS

HELEN AND LARRY EISENBERG

A SECOND HELPING OF OVER 2,000
STATEMENTS
FOR

SIGN BOARDS
BULLETINS AND MAILINGS
SPEECHES
POSTERS
WALL HANGINGS

Lima, Ohio
C.S.S. Publishing Company

MORE BULLETIN BOARD-ERS

4887 ISBN 0-89536-704-1

TABLE OF CONTENTS

INTRODUCTION

The response to our 1973 BULLETIN BOARD-ERS has been very gratifying, and we praise God and thank you and C.S.S. Publishers!

People have become more and more visual-minded, through TV and other influences, and there is a vast increase in outdoor signboards with movable letters for churches, businesses, schools, civic groups.

Once again we're beaming this little book at church use, but anticipate other uses.

Our present outdoor board is a highway marquee read by 20,000 to 40,000 people daily, especially by those on their way to and from Tinker Air Force Base. We have had people come in and inquire about the church from the board, and even to join the church. We believe that beyond any levity or "secular wisdom" we have our board to glorify God and call people to walk with him and with us if they choose.

PEDESTAL BOARDS

These have movable letters and are suitable for lobby, vestibule, narthex for use in churches, schools, businesses, motel and building lobbies and the like. (Two sources: Mishek, Box 109, Waseca, MN 56093 or Hertz Furniture Systems, E. 55 Midland Ave., Paramus, N.J. 07652).

USING THESE QUOTES

We have reduced them, for the most part, by a "billboard technique" to be read at one glance. Most (but not all) should fit on a board with three lines, twenty spaces, or one with four lines, thirteen spaces.

WHAT CAN BOARDERS DO?

They can encourage, inspire, teach, convict, heal, sympathize, cause laughter, improve relationships, protest, express love, encourage prayer, declare, radiate faith, hope . . . be

Biblical, reflect community concerns, announce events, take special stands on issues, reflect the personality of a church, school, business or whatever!

WHAT'S THEIR APPEAL?

Their brevity — you can read in a glance, whether they are used on a board, or as a filler in a church or school or business letter, a short phrase in a message.

On our marquee we mix them up. On one side we'll put what we consider a clever or unusual one, and on the other side one more thoughtful, solid, traditional, Scriptural. Do as you feel best.

Thus, if we use "The Meek Shall Inherit the Work" . . . "A Closed Mouth Catches No Flies" . . . "If God Seems Far Away, Who Moved?" or "Nothing Recedes Like Success!" or maybe "God So Loved That He Didn't Send a Committee," we may run on the other side, "God Is Still In The Rescue Business" or "Take a Spiritual Bath In the Love of God" or perhaps "Jesus Is God's Logo."

Taste . . . objectives . . . theological position will dictate how you use quotes.

TRY THESE USES:

1. As fillers in news sheets, bulletins for church, school, business, newspapers, community news sheets.

2. On secular boards outside schools, restaurants, convenience stores, real estate offices, florists, malls and the like, especially the "punchy" ones.

3. As mentioned earlier, on the indoor "pedestal" boards in vestibules, lobbies, narthexes, halls.

4. Quote them in sermons, talks and lessons.

5. Make posters for classrooms, hall walls, even homes. Have a "poster party" and make a number to be used in weeks and months to come. This can be a project for youth, senior citizens, or classes.

6. Give the book as a gift to ministers, teachers, leaders, friends. Makes a good bathroom reader!

SOME ANGLES WE'VE LEARNED

1. *Attention-getters.* We want people to read our messages, especially the deeper ones. To get interest we put one "catchy" one on one side, a more thoughtful one on the other. Here's one of our combinations! "The Family that Rakes Together Aches Together" with "God Is a Very Present Help In Trouble."

2. *Let It Laugh!* We've had good response to humor, gentle satire, puns, clever twists. "Why Pray When You Can Worry?"

Let it sometimes be your pixie! Richard Cabot said that the balanced life involves "work, play, love, worship." Let it enjoy life! And remember, life is sometimes punny! We got terrific response to our "Bizarre Bazaar."

3. *Take It Seriously.* Change regularly. Don't let the message get too out of date. A bulletin board reflects your personality and character as a church or other organization. Over a period of time, it can tell people what you believe. (The selection of quotes we offer in this book tells what we believe!)

4. *Questions.* Every so often we like to insert questions, giving readers something to think about. Also, they like to fill in the blanks of the subtle ones!

5. *Constantly Consider Your Audience.* What kinds of people will be reading? At times you may want deliberately to beam things at the high school or college crowd . . . the settled church crowd or unchurched, or the bereaved. If a business, you may want to concentrate on punchy, novel phrasing of familiar sayings.

6. *Community Board.* You'll create goodwill by using an outdoor board for high school, college, community events — sports, arts, benefits, emergencies. "Football Is Only A Game — Nevertheless, Beat _____."

7. *Promote with it!* Our marquee draws people by the dozens to our church affairs! Our Mother's Day Out found, when questioning people who applied, that they came not in response to a newspaper ad, for the most part, but from seeing it on the sign! Tell of your activities — youth, senior citizens, general things, bazaars, revivals, seasonal events, special prayer times, church sport activities. We want our board to give the impression of an active, alive church interested also very much in spiritual things.

8. *Vary the Sign.* Don't repeat even good "boarders" for a year or so. (With all this variety, you won't have to.)

9. *Seasonal.* We try to observe the outstanding seasons like New Years, Lincoln's and Washington's Birthdays, Lent and Easter, July 4, Labor Day, Thanksgiving, Advent (especially Christmas) . . . also our own anniversary, etc.

10. *Series.* Sometimes we'll do a series with a connected theme, perhaps using praises from Psalms, a series on love, or perhaps a series using the same words: GOD CARES FOR YOU; GOD CARES FOR YOUR FAMILY; GOD CARES FOR (NAME OF TOWN); GOD CARES WHAT YOU DO AND SAY . . . etc.

CREATING BOARDERS

You develop a knack for it, if you try. Soon you'll find yourself scratching notes on pads, envelopes. In the past few days we got "Jesus Is God's Logo" and "Repent Means About Face." You may want to change the phrasing of some of these in this book.

Our chief sources are the Bible, Christian books (especially from writers who coin phrases, like "Let Go and Let God!"), magazines like *Readers' Digest* and *Quote,* humor sections and humor books. You may go to mottos, familiar sayings, even hymnals: "Give of Your Best To The Master," "Help Somebody Today!"

READ AND MARK

Using this for a spare-time or bathroom reader, just sit and mark in the margins. (Then indicate when it was used.)

And if you like this one, get a copy of the first BULLETIN BOARDERS and do the same with it. We've tried to eliminate duplications, though we may have inadvertently repeated a few. The first book has some good ones!

LET US HEAR FROM YOU!

We'd be glad to have you write us in care of the publisher, and we want to thank especially Wesley T. Runk for his encouragement, and Bill Dickey for helping us to sort and type.

Larry and Helen Eisenberg

WISDOM

SOLOMON'S WISDOM WAS FROM ALL THAT GOOD ADVICE.
FEW ARE FAST ENOUGH TO KEEP UP WITH GOOD INTEN-
TIONS.
HINDSIGHT SHOWS WHAT FORESIGHT COULD HAVE PRE-
VENTED.
NOTHING TAKES THE PLACE OF PERSISTENCE.
NO ONE CAN MEET THE NEEDS OF EVERYONE.
IT'S WRONG TO DO THE RIGHT THING THE WRONG WAY.
THE MORE WE SWEAT FOR PEACE, THE LESS IN WAR.
THERE ARE MANY STARTERS BUT FEW FINISHERS.
WITH GOD YOU'RE NEVER A WRITE-OFF!
GET IT TOGETHER WITH GOD.
DON'T MISS THE SILVER LINING LOOKING FOR GOLD.
ANGELS WHISPER TO THOSE ON WALKS!
THE QUIET ONE MAY HAVE SAID ALL HE KNOWS.
IF LONELY, LOOK WHO BUILT THE WALLS.
YESTERDAY IS A CANCELED CHECK.
SERVICE IS YOUR RENT FOR ROOM ON EARTH.
BURDENS SHARED ARE BURDENS LIGHTENED.
FOR PRIDE'S SAKE COMPARE YOUR KNOWLEDGE WITH THE
VAST STORE.
MANY WOULD BE WORSE IF THE ESTATE HAD BEEN BIGGER.
DON'T CHEAT GOD AND CALL IT ECONOMY.
THE GROUND IS LEVEL BEFORE THE CROSS!
SOME THINK THEY'RE BUSY WHEN THEY'RE ONLY CON-
FUSED.
YOU CAN RUIN THE PRESENT WORRYING ABOUT THE
FUTURE.
NO ONE CAN MEET THE NEEDS OF EVERYONE! EXCEPT GOD.
MUSIC WASHES AWAY THE DUST OF ORDINARY LIFE.
ADULTS LEARN BY TEACHING CHILDREN.
WIT IS A SWORD — YOU SEE AND FEEL THE POINT.
THE EYES ARE THE WINDOWS OF THE SOUL.
HELPING OTHERS IS TIRING BUT REWARDING.
WHETHER YOU BELIEVE IT OR NOT, LAW OF GRAVITY
WORKS!
ORIGINAL THINKING IS LONELY.
THE POOR MAN IS THE ONE WITHOUT A DREAM!

HE WHO CONDEMNS GETS CONDEMNED.
OPPORTUNITIES TAKE SHAPE WITHIN PROBLEMS.
ADAM WORE THE FIRST MASK.
FOR THE BEST FIRE PUT TOGETHER SEVERAL LOGS.
LITTLE LEAKS SINK GREAT SHIPS.
EVERY GUILTY ONE IS HIS OWN HANGMAN.
BE CONTENT WITH WHAT YOU HAVE, BUT NOT WITH WHAT
    YOU ARE.
DIFFICULTIES ARE OFTEN DOORS TO GROWTH.
IT'S LATER THAN YOU THINK.
TACKLE SMALL PROBLEMS BEFORE THEY GROW UP.
WHEN YOU DRINK WATER REMEMBER THE SPRING.
LAWS ARE BASED ON RIGHTS AS WELL AS WRONGS.
BE MODEST: THE FULL HEAD OF WHEAT BENDS.
CARE FOR MINUTES AND HOURS CARE FOR THEMSELVES.
A HAPPY FAMILY IS AN EARLIER HEAVEN.
THE END MAY NOT JUSTIFY THE MEANS.
DOING DRUGS IS GOING INTO CAPTIVITY.
RIGHT IS RIGHT EVEN IF EVERYONE IS AGAINST IT!
PIGS GRUNT ABOUT EVERYTHING.
WHEN YOU LIVE FOR THAT SMALLER THAN SELF, YOU
    SHRINK.
SOME GROW IN RESPONSIBILITY. OTHERS SWELL.
HE WHO SAVES HIS LIFE SHALL LOSE IT!
THE JUDGE IS CONDEMNED WHEN THE GUILTY ARE
    ACQUITTED.
CHARACTER IS WHAT YOU ARE IN THE DARK.
TO BE OPPOSITE IS A FORM OF IMITATION.
LOVE YOUR ENEMIES — THEY TELL YOU YOUR FAULTS.
THE SECURE CAN DO WITHOUT.
ACKNOWLEDGING MISTAKES IS NOT A MISTAKE.
A CLEAR CONSCIENCE IS A VERY SOFT PILLOW.
WHILE LOOKING FOR RAINY DAYS ENJOY THE SUNSHINE.
HE WHO GAMBLES PICKS HIS OWN POCKET.
PLANES RISE BY FLYING INTO THE WIND.
ANGER BLOWS OUT THE LAMP OF THE MIND.
YOU ARE RESPONSIBLE FOR THE FACE YOU DIE WITH.
GOD GLADLY GIVES DIRECTION, BUT NOT ALWAYS
    INSTANTLY.

CIVILIZATION IS THE SLOW PROCESS OF USING IDEAS OF
   MINORITIES.
IT IS EASY TO BE FOR THE RIGHTS OF YOUR OWN MINORITY.
HABITS ARE FIRST COBWEBS, THEN CABLES.
THE UNEXPLORED TODAY IS IN HEARTS AND MINDS.
REAL INTEGRITY NEEDS FEW RULES.
OLD ERROR IS MORE POPULAR THAN NEW TRUTH!
"YOU CAN ALWAYS APOLOGIZE BUT YOU CAN'T ALWAYS
   GET PERMISSION."
WORSHIP, WAIT, AND WORK ALL GO TOGETHER.
NOTHING EXCEEDS LIKE EXCESS.
A THOUSAND FORESTS ARE IN ONE ACORN.
WHAT WE SEND INTO OTHERS' LIVES COMES TO OUR OWN.
SCIENTISTS RESPECT THE GIVEN.
FLOWERS ARE GOD'S BEAUTIFUL THOUGHTS.
GREED SWIFTLY GROWS PIOUS.
STAND WITH THE MINORITY WHEN IT IS RIGHT.
THERE IS NO SUBSTITUTE FOR THE IRREPLACEABLE.
A TWINGE OF CONSCIENCE IS A GIFT OF GOD.
FEW HAVE ENOUGH CHARACTER FOR A LIFE OF IDLENESS.
MOUNTAINS ARE GOD'S MAJESTIC THOUGHTS.
TRUE BEAUTY IS GOD'S HANDWRITING.
KILL TIME AND INJURE ETERNITY.
THE SOUL FORGETTING WHAT GOD PRIZES HAS NO JOY.
SOME ARE SEARCHING FOR GOD AND DON'T KNOW IT.
FOLKS WILL BELIEVE ANYTHING WHISPERED.
HONESTY — FIRST CHAPTER IN BOOK OF WISDOM.
70 YEARS YOUNG IS BETTER THAN 40 YEARS OLD.
SHOOT FOR THE SUN — YOU MAY HIT A STAR.
TO HAVE MORE, WANT LESS.
CIVILIZATIONS DIE WHEN THEY FORGET PEOPLE.
TAKE ONE STEP AT A TIME.
AN OPEN ENEMY DOES MORE GOOD THAN A FALSE FRIEND.
HALF-TRUTH BEGETS TOTAL ERROR!
YOUR SMILE MAY BE SOMEONE'S NECESSITY.
YOU ARE WHAT YOU READ.
TO AN UNJUST GOVERNMENT A MARTYR IS MORE DANGER-
   OUS THAN A REBEL.
THE WORST BLACK EYES ARE SELF-INFLICTED.
DON'T GIVE EXCUSES YOU WOULDN'T ACCEPT.

VARIETY GIVES LIFE SPICE; MONOTONY GIVES THE GROCERIES.

TEMPER GETS YOU INTO TROUBLE — PRIDE KEEPS YOU IN!

POSSESSIONS CAN BE GIFTS THAT JUST DIED!

NOTHING IS POLITICALLY RIGHT AND MORALLY WRONG.

EDUCATION WITHOUT RELIGION MAKES CLEVER DEVILS.

HE WHO IS IMPATIENT WAITS TWICE.

CHANGED ATTITUDES CHANGE CIRCUMSTANCES.

ONLY THE LITTLE BELITTLE.

REMEMBER: LIFE COMES A DAY AT A TIME.

THOSE WHO BRING SUNSHINE TO OTHERS GET IT THEMSELVES.

THERE IS MORE TO LIFE THAN INCREASING ITS SPEED.

THE OPPORTUNITY OF A LIFETIME MAY NOT BE LABELED.

THE UNIVERSE GIVES BACK ACTION FOR ACTION!

CRIMINALS: THOSE WHO HATE NEIGHBORS AS THEMSELVES.

YOU CAN JUDGE A PERSON BY HIS ENEMIES.

YOU CAN TRUST GOD — AND HE'S OVER 30!

IT IS HARD TO SWIM WITH ONE FOOT ON THE GROUND.

WELCOME IDEAS — ONE MAY BE THE KING.

HE IS KIND TO HIMSELF WHO IS KIND TO HIS WIFE.

BETTER TO RISE TO THE OCCASION THAN HIT THE CEILING.

IN ORDER TO FAIL, TRY TO PLEASE EVERYBODY.

WE BECOME LIKE THE THOUGHTS WE HOLD.

ONLY THE DAY DAWNS TO WHICH WE ARE AWAKE.

UNSAID EVIL WORDS SWALLOWED DO NOT HARM THE STOMACH.

PROGRESSIVE SOCIETIES NEED THE ECCENTRIC!

A GRAVEYARD IS MOST PEACEFUL!

TOMORROW MAY NOT BE, BUT YOU HAVE TODAY.

WE APPRECIATE BLESSINGS BY LOSING THEM.

WE ARE NEVER FREE TO ESCAPE THE CONSEQUENCES.

EVERY DAWN BRINGS A FRESH NEW DAY!

NOTHING IS WORTH MORE THAN THIS DAY!

NOBODY GETS UP BEFORE GOD!

FOR PEACE, RESIGN AS GENERAL MGR. OF UNIVERSE.

CLEVERLY SELF-CENTERED IS STILL SELF-CENTERED.

BIRDS FACE THE WIND TO KEEP THEIR FEATHERS IN PLACE!

LIFE'S BEST REWARDS ARE USUALLY NOT BUNCHED!

WANDERLUST IS COSTLY.

NOT MANY GREAT MEN GOT THERE BY DROPPING OUT OF SCHOOL.

THIS IS STILL THE LAND OF OPPORTUNITY.

THE HARDEST THING TO GIVE IS IN.

EASE UP! STRESS COMES FROM MAKING EVERY MINUTE COUNT.

GENIUS IS A TRAIL OF SPARKS FROM A GRINDSTONE!

THE BEST ERASER IS A GOOD NIGHT'S SLEEP.

PEACEMAKERS DROP ARGUMENTS, TAKE UP PRAYER.

TRUE FREEDOM IS FRAGILE AND COSTLY. — Billy Graham

TODAY'S FREEDOM NEEDS CHRIST'S DISCIPLINE.

ALL FREEDOM INCLUDES LIMITATIONS.

WE ARE LIBERATED ONLY WHEN GOD HAS HIS WAY.

MEN RATTLE THEIR CHAINS TO SHOW THEY'RE FREE!

YOU'RE FREE ONLY IF FREE TO MAKE MISTAKES!

THERE ARE 35 MILLION LAWS TO ENFORCE THE TEN COM—MANDMENTS!

INNOCENCE IS NO GUARANTEE OF NICE TREATMENT!

ART AND MORALITY DRAW THE LINE SOMEWHERE.

REACH OUT AND TOUCH SOMEONE!

DIAMONDS — COAL THAT STAYED IN THERE!

MAKE FRIENDS BEFORE YOU NEED THEM! — Estep

ALL PEOPLE WANT TO BE TREATED AS HUMAN BEINGS.

IN FRIENDSHIP DEPTH RETURNS DEPTH.

TO THE CRITICAL THE WHOLE WORLD IS AT FAULT.

YOU CAN FAST SPIRITUALLY BY LEAVING OFF CRITICISM.

CRITICISM IS THE FRUIT OF RESENTMENT.

LIKE RAIN, CRITICISM SHOULD ENCOURAGE GROWTH WITHOUT DESTROYING ROOTS.

IF YOU MUST SUFFER, DO IT FOR SOMETHING POSITIVE!

KIND WORDS BRING KIND ECHOES!

AS WITH MOTORS, SOMETHING'S WRONG WHEN WE KNOCK.

NORTH POLE EXPEDITION PROVES NOBODY IS SITTING ON TOP OF WORLD.

SOME THINK HANDWRITING ON WALL IS FORGERY.

HELD HANDS FEEL SUPPORT.

KINDNESS IS CHRISTIANITY IN WORK CLOTHES.

THE OPTIMIST SEES THE BRIGHT SIDE OF YOUR PROBLEM.

WEIGH NEIGHBOR IN SAME BALANCE AS YOURSELF.

YOU'RE YOUNG ONLY ONCE: THEN YOU NEED A NEW EXCUSE.

BUT FOR FAITH WE COULDN'T EAT HASH IN SAFETY!

HORSEPOWER WAS SAFER WHEN ONLY HORSES HAD IT!

TO FORGET TROUBLES WEAR SHOES A SIZE TOO SMALL.

TODAY — SEND OUT ONLY KINDLY **THOUGHTS**.

A SUBMARINE IS A SHIP THAT SINKS ON **PURPOSE**.

TO AVOID CRITICISM, SAY NOTHING, DO NOTHING, BE NOTHING!

HANDSOME APPLES ARE SOMETIMES SOUR!

FRIENDSHIP IS BOUGHT WITH **FRIENDSHIP**.

YOU'RE NOT RICH ENOUGH TO DO WITHOUT A NEIGHBOR!

THE DOOR TO THE HUMAN HEART OPENS FROM THE **INSIDE**.

A FRIEND IS ONE WITH WHOM YOU DARE TO BE **YOURSELF**.

COMMIT, TRUST, AND WATCH THE RESULTS!

TROUBLE IS OPPORTUNITY IN WORK CLOTHES!

PEOPLE SELDOM LOSE JOBS BECAUSE THEY DON'T **DRINK**.

NONE ARE SO BLIND AS THOSE WHO WILL NOT **SEE**.

BLESSED ARE THOSE WHO DROP ARGUMENTS FOR PEACE.

SOW COURTESY AND REAP **FRIENDSHIP**.

PLANT KINDNESS, GATHER **LOVE**.

PEOPLE RESPOND MORE TO HOW YOU FEEL THAN WHAT YOU SAY.

SOME WOULD RATHER BE RIGHT THAN **PLEASANT**.

A FRIEND SEES THROUGH YOU, BUT STILL ENJOYS THE SHOW!

TO DISCOVER YOUR FAULTS, GET MARRIED!

HE'S GROWING UP WHEN HE LOOKS AT GIRLS LIKE CHOCOLATE CHIP COOKIES!

SELFISHNESS IS THE ROOT OF ALL **EVIL**.

YOU'RE OLD WHEN YOU TAKE ESCALATOR TO **BASEMENT**.

ALARM CLOCKS ARE UNPOPULAR — THEY WAKE PEOPLE UP!

TO LIGHTEN YOUR LOAD, LIFT THAT OF ANOTHER.

PRETENDING RICHES CAN KEEP YOU POOR.

ENTHUSIASM IS EASIER THAN OBEDIENCE.

REPENT: ABOUT FACE!

MAN IS THE ONLY ANIMAL THAT BLUSHES!

BEST LEVEL TO LIVE ON — YOUR VERY BEST!

WHAT YOU DISH OUT YOU GET BACK!

FIFTY DISEASES COME FROM BAD THINKING!
WORD OF ADVICE: DON'T GIVE IT!
ENEMIES GIVE CRITICISM NOT PROVIDED BY FRIENDS.
BLESSED ARE THE GENTLE.
IF YOU WANT HENS TO LAY, YOU MUST BEAR THEIR CACKLING!
POISE IS TO BE ILL-AT-EASE INCONSPICUOUSLY.
CHARACTER SHOWS BY CRITICISMS YOU FORGIVE.
OPTIMISM CAN BE SEEING TOO MUCH IN EVERYTHING.
WORDS OF COMFORT ARE THE OLDEST THERAPY.
FIND GOOD IN OTHERS.
A HAPPY MARRIAGE IS WORLD'S BEST BARGAIN.
OPTIMIST: A GROOM WHO THINKS HE HAS NO BAD HABITS.
"ONE OF THESE DAYS" IS NONE OF THESE DAYS.
PESSIMISTS COME FROM FINANCING OPTIMISTS.
OPTIMISTS GET RICH BUYING OUT PESSIMISTS.
TO HEAT UP AN ARGUMENT, RUB TWO FENDERS TOGETHER.
LOOK BEYOND LABELS TO SEE WHO A PERSON IS.
A LACK OF ENTHUSIASM IS ALSO CONTAGIOUS.
KINDNESS CONVERTS MORE THAN ELOQUENCE.
A RAINY VACATION IS LIKE TWO WEEKS IN A CAR WASH.
YOUR HEAD ACHES NOT WHEN COMFORTING ANOTHER.
CRITICISM IS OFTEN AN ESCAPE.
PESSIMISTS CALL TRAFFIC SIGNALS "STOP LIGHTS".
OPTIMISM CAN TURN TO GOLD WHAT IT TOUCHES.
IF CRITICIZED, YOU HAVE PROBABLY DONE SOMETHING WORTHWHILE.
REPUTATION: CHARACTER MINUS WHAT YOU'VE BEEN CAUGHT DOING.
IF WE'RE NOT SHOULDER TO SHOULDER, WE'RE NOT HEART TO HEART.
ARGUMENT: THE LONGEST DISTANCE BETWEEN TWO POINTS OF VIEW.
POISE: UNRUFFLED WHEN MAKING SAME MISTAKE TWICE.
MORALLY, THE MIND IS THE "HILL HOLDING THE PASS."
THE LUST FOR POWER IS ROOTED IN WEAKNESS.
VISIT A FRIEND OFTEN; WEEDS CHOKE UNUSED PATHS.

GOD

HE IS JEHOVAH, THE GOD ALMIGHTY!
BE OPEN AND EAGER FOR A FRESH VIEW OF GOD!
GOD WITHIN, GOD AROUND, GOD BELOW, GOD ABOVE!
MAN IS ONLY FREE IN GOD, THE SOURCE OF HIS FREEDOM.
THE SECRET OF GOD IS WITH THOSE WHO REVERE HIM.
GOD IS CONCERNED ABOUT SOULS . . . AND RHEUMATISM.
GOD COMES THROUGH PEOPLE, HORIZONTALLY — ONE TO
    ONE.
WHEN WE GIVE UP, GOD IS JUST BEGINNING!
WHAT WE GIVE AWAY IN GOD'S NAME COMES BACK
    BLESSED.
GOD IS EVERYWHERE LOOKING FOR HANDS TO USE.
BLESSED ARE THOSE WHO STAND FOR GOD'S RIGHTEOUS —
    NESS.
THE HAND OF THE LORD IS NOT SHORTENED: HE CAN SAVE!
ONLY IN GOD CAN YOU FIND WHO YOU ARE!
LET GOD DEAL WITH YOUR STRESS.
YOU CANNOT SERVE GOD AND MONEY.
THE GOD WHO CREATED ALL IS LOVE.
DON'T GET RIGHT WITH GOD "SOMEDAY" — NOW!
LET YOUR WHOLE LIFE SING TO THE GLORY OF GOD!
GOD IS THE ONLY ONE WHO CAN HANDLE RESENTMENT.
GOD MADE US FOR HIMSELF; WE REST ONLY IN HIM.
GOD WILL ALWAYS HELP YOU LAND ON YOUR FEET!
IN GOD LIFE IS FULL OF SPONTANEOUS, JOYFUL UNCER —
    TAINTY!
GOD SEES TO IT THAT EVERY TEMPTATION HAS A WAY OUT.
LITTLE IS MUCH WHEN GOD IS IN IT!
GOD IS REAL! ASK ANY WHO KNOW HIM.
GOD OFTEN STARTS WITH THE INFINITELY SMALL!
"GOD, STAB MY SOUL FIERCELY WITH OTHERS' PAIN."
WITH GOD YOU'RE ON SOLID GROUND IN A SHAKY
    WORLD.
GOD WORKS ESPECIALLY IN TROUBLE.
GOD WILL ALWAYS GIVE A BOUNTIFUL SUPPLY OF WISDOM.
GOD WILL SUPPLY ALL YOUR REAL NEEDS.

BE TO GOD WHAT HANDS ARE TO A MAN.

GOD'S FIVE BIG WORDS: HUMBLE, HONEST, CONFESS, RE-
PENT, FORGIVE.

YOU CAN'T OUTGIVE GOD!

GOD WORKS THROUGH PEOPLE WHO WORK.

THE WAY TO TEST GOD IS TO TRUST HIM!

GOD HELPS THOSE WHO CAN'T HELP THEMSELVES.

GOD IS LIGHT — IN HIM IS NO DARKNESS AT ALL — Jn. 1:5.

GOD IS NOT AN ELECTIVE.

EVERY BELIEVER IS GOD'S MIRACLE.

YOU'LL NEVER GET RIGHT WITH GOD ANY YOUNGER!

GOD WORKS ESPECIALLY IN TROUBLE.

GIVE GOD YOUR WEAKNESS FOR HIS STRENGTH.

TAKE YOUR SPIRITUAL WOUNDS TO GOD.

YOUR HELP COMES FROM GOD WHO MADE HEAVEN AND
EARTH!

CORRECT RESPONSE TO GOD: "HERE I AM — SEND ME!"

NOTHING HAPPENS WITHOUT GOD'S KNOWLEDGE.

BE SILENT AND LET GOD MOLD YOU!

GOD IS SO GOOD!

IN THE CENTER OF TROUBLE, GOD REVIVES.

WITH GOD, LOVE, TRUST, WAIT AND SEE.

GOD CAN MAKE YOU WHOLE!

TO STEER SAFELY THROUGH EVERY STORM, FIX TRUST ON
GOD.

WHEN GOD SAYS SO, LAUNCH INTO THE DEEP!

IT'S HARD TO SERVE GOD AND STATUS.

TO HEAR GOD'S CALL YOU HAVE TO BE IN HEARING DIS—
TANCE.

GOD IS EVERYWHERE LOOKING FOR HANDS TO USE.

THE BASIC HUMAN SIN: PLAYING GOD!

GOD IS STILL IN THE RESCUE BUSINESS.

GOD IS THE GOD OF 11:59!

THE KINGDOM OF GOD IS WITHIN YOU.

GOODBYE IS SHORT FOR "GOD BE WITH YOU!"

GOD IS GREATER THAN ANY PROBLEMS.

GOD'S MERCIES ARE NEW EVERY MORNING.

GOD WILL REPAY THOSE WHO DESERVE IT.

WITH GOD EVERYBODY IS SOMEBODY.

THIS IS THE DAY THAT THE LORD HAS MADE.

GOD FORGIVES WRONGS, HEALS OUR DISEASES.

EVERY GOOD AND PERFECT GIFT IS FROM ABOVE.

GOD BIDS YOU GO WHEN YOU WOULD STAY.

THERE'S ALWAYS PLENTY OF TIME TO WORSHIP GOD!

"HE WHO CARES FOR THE POOR LENDS TO GOD." — Prov. 20:17.

CORRECT RESPONSE TO GOD: "HERE I AM — SEND ME!"

TAKE A SPIRITUAL BATH IN THE LOVE OF GOD.

GOD OVER ALL, IN ALL, THROUGH ALL.

GOD IS PREPARING HIS HEROES.

"EVEN WHEN YOUR HAIR IS WHITE, I WILL TAKE CARE OF YOU" — GOD'S PROMISE.

GOD IS STILL PUBLISHING!

GOD WILL HEAL YOUR MEMORIES IF YOU'LL LET HIM.

THE ONLY WAY TO TEST GOD IS TO TRUST HIM!

BETTER THAN ANGER — LEAVE IT TO GOD.

ONLY GOD CAN CURE SOUL-SICKNESS.

SOMETIMES GOD DENIES PEACE TO GIVE YOU HIS GLORY!

GIVE YOUR BAD STUFF TO GOD.

GOD IS NOT A COSMIC BELL-BOY.

GOD IS SLOW TO ANGER, PLENTEOUS IN MERCY.

GOD KEEPS HIS PROMISES.

GOD GIVES US SUPER STRENGTH.

LET GO AND LET GOD!

OFTEN "HOW" AND "WHEN" ARE GOD'S MYSTERIES.

YOU CAN'T BE WRONG WITH HUMANITY AND RIGHT WITH GOD.

WHEN WE COME TO THE END OF SELF, GOD CAN GET TO WORK.

GOD WANTS TO LOOSEN OUR BONDS TO THINGS.

GIVE GOD'S BLESSINGS BACK TO HIM AS LOVE GIFTS.

THE ETERNAL GOD IS YOUR REFUGE.

BE HONEST WITH GOD!

TRUST GOD WITH YOUR TOMORROWS.

GOD ASKS GROWTH, NOT PERFECTION.

THERE'S INNER PEACE IN KNOWING THAT GOD IS IN CON—TROL.

BE THANKFUL TO GOD AND BLESS HIS NAME.

GIVE GOD YOUR ANXIETY.

GOD COMFORTS US TO MAKE US COMFORTERS.

WITH GOD YOU HAVE THE WISDOM OF TEN BILLION YEARS!

RIGHT NOW YOU'RE UNDER GOD'S WATCHFUL GAZE!
GO AGAINST GOD'S GRAIN AND GET SPLINTERS!
WHEN GOD GETS US ALONE HE CAN BEGIN TO EXPOUND.
BECAUSE GOD LOVES, HE SOMETIMES CHASTISES!
GOD GIVES US A SPIRIT OF POWER, LOVE, DISCIPLINE.
GOD SUPPLIES FROM THE WELL OF HIS WORD.
OBEY GOD OR FACE THE CONSEQUENCES.
GOD SO LOVED THAT HE DIDN'T SEND A COMMITTEE.
GOD IS SO GOOD!
HE RESTORES YOUR SOUL.
GIVE GOD THE GLORY DUE HIS NAME.
THE UNIVERSE IS CENTERED ONLY IN GOD.
GOD'S FAVOR LASTS FOR LIFE.
HELP GOD PUSH BACK THE DARKNESS!
GOD SO LOVED THE WORLD. IT SAYS, INTERESTINGLY, NOT
    "THE CHURCH."
THE BEATITUDES: EIGHT PATHS TO KNOWING GOD. (Matt. 5)
FOR GOD'S ANSWERS, WORK AT LISTENING.
GOD ISN'T AFRAID OF ANYTHING.
GOD LOVES YOU AS YOU ARE.
GOD DIDN'T STOP PUBLISHING WHEN HIS BOOK WENT TO
    PRESS.
GOD COMFORTS THE AFFLICTED, AFFLICTS THE COMFORT-
    ABLE.
GOD LOVES YOU WHERE YOU ARE, AS YOU ARE!
TRY CONFESSING YOUR OWN NEEDS TO GOD.
GOD HOLDS HANDS.
GOD HELPS US DO GREATER THINGS.
GOD MEANS WHAT HE SAYS.
GOD'S GRACE IS SUFFICIENT FOR YOU.
GOD DOESN'T GIVE ADVICE AND RUN.
THE LORD WANTS TO BLESS YOU AND KEEP YOU.
GOD HELPS THOSE WHO CAN'T HELP THEMSELVES.
SAY YES TO LIFE AS GOD INTENDS IT!
WORSHIP IS ACTIVE RESPONSE TO GOD.
ONLY GOD CAN MAKE A TREE.
TREAT OTHERS AS GOD WOULD TREAT THEM.
GOD'S JUDGMENTS ARE IMPARTIAL!
GOD LOVES THE UNLOVELY.
GOD IS IN THE BROKEN-HEART-MENDING BUSINESS.
NO EDUCATION IS "LIBERAL" UNLESS GOD IS CENTRAL.

12

GOD FORGIVES INSTANTLY.
GOD'S PROTECTION IS 24 HOURS A DAY.
CONFESSON IS GOD'S DETERGENT.
LEANING ON GOD IS LIKE LEARNING TO FLOAT.
GOD PROVIDES WAYS OUT WHEN THERE ARE NONE.
GOD'S PEACE HELPS COPE WITH CONFLICT.
GOD RESTED THE 7TH DAY — WE NEED IT TOO!
ASK GOD TO BLESS YOUR WORK BUT NOT TO *DO* IT.
HAS YOUR LIFE EVER SAID YES TO GOD?
YOU CAN FIND DIRECTON BY SIMPLY ASKING GOD.
GOD'S GIVING KNOWS NO LIMITS.
DO ALL TO THE GLORY OF GOD!
GOD IS A SPIRITUAL GARBAGE COLLECTOR.
NO LIFE IS TOO BROKEN FOR GOD TO REPAIR.
OUR NATIVE LAND IS THE KINGDOM OF GOD!
THE WORLD WILL BE SAVED ONLY BY THE HAND OF GOD.
PERFECT FREEDOM IS IN GOD'S SERVICE.
WHEN GOD SAYS, "DO IT" — DO IT!
GOD LOVES AS IF THERE WERE ONLY ONE TO LOVE.
FATHERS WILL PAY FOR THINKING LITTLE OF GOD!
GOD ISN'T DEAD, BUT WITH SOME, UNEMPLOYED!
WHEN DARKNESS FOLLOWS A VISION FROM GOD — WAIT.
WITHOUT GOD THE RICH ARE THE POOREST!
IN WORSHP I BRING MY LIFE TO GOD.
GOD IS A WORKING FATHER.
WE'RE NOT ALL THE SAME, BUT GOD LOVES US ALL.
GOD CALLS FOR TOTAL COMMITMENT OF TOTAL MAN.
I KNOW NOT WHAT THE FUTURE BRINGS BUT KNOW WHO
    HOLDS THE FUTURE.
CHOOSE A PATH THAT LEADS TO GOD.
GOD'S LOVE SAVES.
WITH GOD, ALL THINGS ARE POSSIBLE!
**TODAY, TOO, GOD NEEDS TO COMMUNICATE WITH HIS
    PEOPLE.**
GOD IS STILL SAVING WHAT HE HAS CREATED.
LIFE WITHOUT GOD IS EMPTY.
ETERNAL LIFE IS A GIFT OF GOD.
"TRUST GOD WITH THE CONFIDENCE OF A CHILD ASLEEP."
GOOD NEWS — GOD IS LIKE CHRIST!
EVERY COMMON BUSH IS AFIRE WITH GOD.

GOD IS WITH YOU WHEREVER YOU GO.
TO RECEIVE GOD'S MERCY JUST HOLD OUT YOUR HANDS!
THE PURE IN HEART **DO** SEE GOD.
GOD CANNOT HONOR OUR REBELLION.
GOD CAN HEAL YOUR HEARTACHE! GIVE IT OVER.
GOD RENEWS YOUR MIND.
WE ARE GOD'S WORKMANSHIP.
GOD SAYS, "LOVE, AND LEAVE JUDGING TO ME."
GOD WON'T LET YOU FEEL RIGHT AND DO WRONG!
INTERESTING: ATHEISTS TALK THE MOST ABOUT GOD!
GOD'S PROPHETS WIN NO POPULARITY CONTESTS!
ON THE SHELF? GOD'S THERE TOO!
TIME FOR GOD IS LIFE'S ONLY LASTING INVESTMENT.
GOD'S MERCY IS EVERLASTING.
ONLY AN EMPTIED LIFE HAS ROOM FOR GOD.
GOD BECAME MAN THAT MAN MIGHT BECOME LIKE GOD.
THIS IS STILL OUR FATHER'S WORLD!
ALL THINGS ARE POSSIBLE WITH GOD!
IF YOU HAVE TOO MUCH, THE LORD WANTS YOU TO SHARE.
GOD IS AN "EVERYTHING" GOD, NOT A "SOME THINGS"
    GOD.
GOD PITY YOU IF YOUR DREAMS ARE DEAD.
GOD-IN-US MAKES US SEEK GOD!
LIFE IS EMPTY WITHOUT GOD!
IN GOD IS OUR UNITY.
IT IS FOLLY TO SAY "THERE IS NO GOD!"
GOD CARES.
GOD SPEAKS BEST TO UNSTOPPED EARS.
BLESSED IS THE ONE WHO TRUSTS IN GOD!
GOD DOESN'T TAKE A VACATION.
GOD KNOWS YOU BY NAME!
THE WORLD WILL BE SAVED ONLY BY THE HAND OF GOD.
WHERE I AM, GOD IS!
YOU CAN'T FOLLOW EQUALLY "COMMON SENSE" AND GOD.
GUILT IS TOO HEAVY: GIVE IT TO GOD!
GOD NEVER GIVES ANYTHING ACCIDENTALLY.
IN GOD IS OUR UNITY.
THE LOST ARE THOSE WHO REFUSE GOD'S LOVE.
GOD IS THE ONLY ONE WHO CAN HANDLE YOUR RESENT-
    MENTS.

ONLY GOD CAN KEEP DIRECTION CENTRAL.
GOD'S BUSINESS IS SELLING DREAMS.
THE GREAT GOD ALMIGHTY LOVES YOU.
GOD EXAMINES MOTIVE AS WELL AS DEED.
GOD IS NOT SHOCKED BY YOUR SINS! TALK WITH HIM!
WHEN GOD BRINGS A BLANK SPACE — WAIT.
GOD'S PROTECTION SYSTEM IS 24 HOURS A DAY.
HEARING GOD'S CALL DEPENDS ON THE STATE OF MY
    EARS.
IF GOD IS FATHER, ALL ARE BROTHERS!
LET GOD INTO THE SECRET PLACES OF YOUR SOUL.
GOD DESIRES COMPASSION MORE THAN SACRIFICE!
ONLY GOD CAN BUILD WELL WITH STUMBLING BLOCKS.
GOD IS THE SAME YESTERDAY, TODAY, AND FOREVER!
FIRST THERE WAS GOD!
WHEN WE HEAR ONLY OURSELVES WE CAN'T HEAR GOD!
GOD IS EVERYWHERE LOOKING FOR HANDS TO USE.
LOOK FOR GOD'S MIRACLE TODAY!
GOD IS THE HELP OF THE HELPLESS.
GOD FREES OUR SOULS NOT FROM BUT INTO DUTY.
DON'T WAIT TO BE SUPERNATURALLY INSPIRED TO GET TO
    GOD'S WORK.
TO HEAR GOD'S CALL, TUNE IN!
GOD CAN MAKE GOLD FROM JUNK!
AT THE HEART OF SILENCE, THERE IS GOD!
TIME FOR GOD IS LIFE'S LASTING INVESTMENT.
GOD WANTS GROWTH IN CHRISTLIKE LIVING.
IN EARTH'S COMMON THINGS GOD STANDS REVEALED.
CONSECRATE EMOTIONS TO SERVING GOD!
TURN GOD LOOSE ON YOUR AGENDA FOR TODAY.
NEVER RUN BEFORE GOD'S GUIDANCE.
PUT GOD FIRST OR YOU LOSE!
WE CAN PRAISE GOD IN THE MOST HOPELESS SITUATIONS.
GOD IS NOT AFRAID OF YOUR DOUBT!
GOD JUDGES HOW WE USE OUR POTENTIAL.
DELIBERATELY TURN YOUR IMAGINATION TO GOD!
GOD LOVES GRAY HAIR. HIS IS WHITE.
THE MORE OBEDIENT TO GOD, THE MORE REAL HE IS!
AMERICA! AMERICA! GOD SHED HIS GRACE ON THEE!
WORSHIP IS GIVING GOD THE BEST HE HAS GIVEN YOU.

OBEDIENCE: TURN BACK ON PROBLEM, FACE TO GOD.
YOU DON'T HAVE TO TRY EVERYTHING BEFORE TRYING
GOD!

16

JESUS

JESUS STILL MAKES HOUSE CALLS.
EVEN JESUS SOMETIMES SAID "NO."
CHRIST IS SO UNEXPECTEDLY, INCREDIBLY RIGHT!
JESUS WAS THE PERSONAL EVIDENCE OF GOD!
OVERWHELMING VICTORY IS YOURS THROUGH CHRIST.
JESUS SAID IF YOU HAVE AUGHT AGAINST ANY, FORGIVE.
DENY YOURSELF, TAKE YOUR CROSS, FOLLOW JESUS.
IN CHRIST YOU ARE A NEW CREATION — OLD IS GONE, NEW
    HAS COME.
JESUS LOVES US OUT OF OUR SIN!
GOD GIVES FULL HUMILITY WHEN YOU ACCEPT CHRIST'S
    FULL HUMANITY.
IF YOU LOVE JESUS, TITHE — ANYBODY CAN HONK!
CHRIST REQUIRES CHRISTIANS TO FORGIVE UNCONDITION-
    ALLY.
CHRIST DRAWS A CIRCLE THAT TAKES EVERYBODY IN.
JESUS WAS SO GREAT HE COULD BE GENTLE!
TAKE THE CROSS AS SERIOUSLY AS JESUS DID!
CAST YOUR CARES ON HIM; HE CARES FOR YOU.
HE SAVED OTHERS; WE SEEK TO SAVE OURSELVES.
JESUS SAID, "GO AND SIN NO MORE."
THE WORD BECAME — NOT REASON — BUT FLESH!
JESUS IS IN THE HUNGRY, THE NAKED, THE PRISONER.
TO ENTHRONE CHRIST, DETHRONE YOURSELF.
IN CHRIST DIFFERENCES DON'T DESTROY FELLOWSHIP.
TURN IT OVER TO JESUS — EVERYTHING'S GONNA BE ALL
    RIGHT.
ON GANDHI'S WALL: "HE IS OUR PEACE."
THE LORD IS MY HEALER.
JESUS STANDS AT YOUR DOOR AND KNOCKS.
WHOEVER LOSES HIS LIFE FOR CHRIST'S SAKE FINDS IT.
CHRIST'S PEACE LAUGHS IN THE FACE OF DEATH!
"JESUS, I DIDN'T KNOW I WAS HUNGRY TILL I MET YOU."
JESUS IS LORD OF ALL OR NOT LORD AT ALL.
HE WILL NEVER LEAVE YOU NOR FORSAKE YOU.
CAST ALL YOUR CARE ON HIM; **HE CARES FOR YOU.**
JESUS IS THE FOCUS OF GOD IN HUMAN HISTORY.

HE WILL GIVE YOU REST.

BOIL DOWN PSYCHOLOGY AND YOU GET THE SERMON ON THE MOUNT.

JESUS IN GETHSEMANE: "THY WILL BE DONE!"

CHRIST OPENS THE DOOR TO A NEW LIFE.

JESUS: "YOU'RE MY FRIEND IF YOU DO MY COMMAND-MENTS."

JESUS SAYS, "COME!"

WHAT JESUS TAUGHT, HE DID.

CHRIST CAN END YOUR SEARCH FOR IDENTITY!

JESUS IS THE DIVINE YES.

RENEWAL BEGINS ONLY WITH JESUS CHRIST.

JESUS LOVES YOU!

J-O-Y IS JESUS, OTHERS, YOURSELF.

JESUS FREES YOU FROM BEING SPIRITUALLY BEDRIDDEN.

BELIEVE ON CHRIST AND YOU SHALL BE SAVED!

IN THE PURE SOUL CHRIST IS BORN ANEW FROM DAY TO DAY.

GOD VISITED THIS PLANET IN THE PERSON OF JESUS.

JESUS TURNS QUESTION MARKS INTO EXCLAMATION POINTS!

THE LORD WASHED HIS DISCIPLES' FEET.

JESUS TEACHES US TO LOVE PERSONS, NO MATTER WHAT!

JESUS DIDN'T LIKE LEGALISTIC NIT-PICKING!

JESUS CAME TO SET CAPTIVES FREE –- FROM SATAN. LET HIM.

JESUS PAID TAXES.

JESUS IS THE AUTHOR OF FAITH; READ HIS BOOK.

JESUS LOVED PEOPLE OUT OF THEIR SIN.

JESUS SAYS, "CHOOSE RIGHT NOW!"

JESUS IS THE WORD BECOME FINAL.

JESUS: "ASK ANYTHING IN MY NAME AND I WILL DO IT."

"I WAS GOING TO WASTE, BUT JESUS RECYCLED ME."

THE GOOD NEWS BEGINS WITH JESUS!

JESUS BRINGS TIDINGS OF COMFORT AND JOY.

LORD, LET ME NOT LIVE TO BE USELESS — FOR CHRIST'S SAKE.

THE BEST TRIP IS WITH JESUS.

JESUS DOES NOT INTEND THAT WE BE SHORTCHANGED IN WHAT WE NEED.

JESUS CAN CHANGE YOUR SELF-HATE.

LAY YOUR TROUBLED LIFE AT THE FEET OF CHRIST.

CHRIST CAN HELP YOU BE O.K.

VICTORY IS YOURS THROUGH CHRIST WHO DIED FOR YOU.

WITH CHRIST WE ARE MORE THAN CONQUERORS!

CAST YOUR CARE ON HIM WHO CARES FOR YOU.

JESUS: "COME TO ME AND I WILL GIVE YOU REST."

"HE WHO LOSES HIS LIFE FOR MY SAKE WILL FIND IT!" —
JESUS.

WHAT JESUS DID HE EXPECTS US TO DO!

JESUS IS OUR PLUMB LINE.

CHRIST LOVED THE CHURCH AND GAVE HIMSELF TO MAKE
HER HOLY.

CHRIST PREVENTS SUCCUMBING TO MEANINGLESSNESS.

JESUS: "YOU'RE SOMEBODY."

MAKE ONLY THE CHANGES CHRIST WANTS IN YOU.

LEARN TO LOVE CHRIST PERSONALLY.

CHRIST OFFERS CAUSES IN WHICH TO FORGET SELF.

JESUS WROTE DIVINE CHECKS TO COVER OUR "OVER-
DRAFTS."

MORE THAN ONCE JESUS SAID, "YOUR FAITH MAKES YOU
WELL!"

THE GOLDEN RULE IS GREAT BECAUSE OF WHO SAID IT.

EVEN A COWARD CAN PRAISE CHRIST.

JESUS LOVES US. THIS WE KNOW FOR THE BIBLE TELLS US
SO!

JESUS' COMMAND: "LOVE ONE ANOTHER AS I HAVE LOVED
YOU."

JESUS GIVES DEEPER JOY!

CHRIST SENT AWAY ONLY THOSE FULL OF THEMSELVES.

JESUS DIDN'T FIGHT SIN BY AVOIDING SINNERS.

OF THREE CRUCIFIED, TWO DESERVED IT.

WE BECOME MEMBERS OF JESUS' FAMILY WHEN WE OBEY.

JESUS DIDN'T RUN!

GOD'S LOVE COST HIM JESUS' LIFE.

GOD WILL SUPPLY ALL YOUR NEEDS ACCORDING TO HIS
RICHES IN GLORY.

WINDS AND WAVES STILL KNOW HIS VOICE.

IN CHRIST YOU ARE A NEW CREATION.

JESUS IS GOD'S LOGO.

CORRECT THIS: HEAR LORD, THY SERVANT SPEAKETH.

GOOD NEWS; GOD IS LIKE CHRIST.
JESUS GOT HIS ROBE DIRTY!
CHRIST CAN DELIVER FROM A LIFE OF DESPERATION.
WHAT A FRIEND WE HAVE IN JESUS!
JESUS IS THE WORD OF GOD!
"JESUS DIDN'T DIE FOR STAINED GLASS WINDOWS."
JESUS CALLS US: WE DON'T NEED A PHONE TO TALK.
JESUS HEADS GOD'S RESCUE PLAN.
IN CHRIST IS LIFE.
LET HIM TAKE STRAIN AND STRESS FROM OUR SOUL.
JESUS ASKS US TO CONFESS FAITH IN HIM BEFORE MEN.
WITH CHRIST NEUTRALITY IS NOT POSSIBLE.
JESUS CHANGED PEOPLE BY SIMPLE LOVE.
NO BURDEN IS TOO HEAVY FOR HIM TO BEAR.
JESUS IS NOT CALLING US TO MOST OF WHAT WE'RE
    DOING.
JESUS: "I HAVE OVERCOME THE WORLD."
WHEREVER GOD BUILDS A CHURCH SATAN ERECTS A
    CHAPEL. — MARTIN LUTHER
LOSE YOUR LIFE FOR HIS SAKE AND YOU'LL FIND IT.
JESUS WAS LIKE — AND IS — GOD!
CHRIST IN THE HEART WILL BE SEEN LOOKING OUT
    WINDOWS.
WHEN WE NEED SAVING FROM ANYTHING JESUS IS READY.
LIKE FATHER, LIKE SON!
CHRIST IS OUR BRIDGE.
JESUS DIDN'T PAINT UTOPIA BUT SAID: THE KINGDOM'S IN
    YOU!
JESUS GIVES INNER PEACE THAT CIRCUMSTANCES WON'T
    SHAKE.
JESUS WAS BORN IN A LOW-INCOME HOME.
TRY SEEING CHRIST IN THOSE WHO DIFFER WITH YOU.
STAND ON JESUS' ROCK WHEN FLOODS COME.
ACCEPT GIFTS OR CROSS GRACIOUSLY — JESUS DID!
WHAT BLOOD TYPE DID JESUS HAVE?

HOLY/UNHOLY SPIRIT

YOUR BODY IS THE TEMPLE OF YOUR SPIRIT.
THE HOLY SPIRIT PRODUCES LOVE, JOY, PEACE, PATIENCE,
KINDNESS, GOODNESS, FAITHFULNESS, GENTLENESS,
SELF-CONTROL.
"MY SPIRIT IS WILLING, BUT METABOLISM IS WEAK!"
MOST POWERFUL WEAPON — SOUL ON FIRE!
THOSE LED BY THE SPIRIT ARE SONS OF GOD.
A TRUE SPIRITUAL EXPERIENCE CORRECTS FAULTS OF CHAR-
ACTER.
SATAN KEEPS SCHOOL FOR NEGLECTED CHILDREN.
NEW SPIRITUAL BIRTH TURNS HATE TO LOVE.
SATAN CAN ONLY SUGGEST.
THE WINDS OF THE SPIRIT BLOW: LIFT YOUR SAILS!
SATAN ONLY GOES WHERE HE'S WELCOME.
TEMPTATION SAYS, "JUST THIS ONCE."
DISCOURAGEMENT IS OF SATAN.
SATAN LOVES GENERALITIES AND POSTPONED ACTION.
RESENTMENT IS CANCER OF THE SPIRIT.
SATAN BINDS AND BLINDS MEN.
THE HOLY SPIRIT IS THE WORD BECOME DYNAMIC.
SELF-CONTEMPT IS ALWAYS FROM SATAN.
SATAN'S CARROTS ARE HALF-TRUTHS.
IN YOU THERE'S A WORLD SERIES -- HOLY VS UNHOLY
SPIRIT.
RESIST SATAN AND HE WILL FLEE FROM YOU.
AWE AND ADORATION TURN US FROM PREOCCUPATION
WITH OURSELVES.
SATAN SEEKS PROCRASTINATION.
MOST WOULD BE A MESS WITHOUT THE HOLY SPIRIT!
SATAN WANTS YOU TO DISOBEY GOD.
THE SPIRIT OF TRUTH GUIDES IN ALL TRUTH.
DESIRE SPIRITUAL GIFTS.
SATAN WANTS "MODERATES", NOT TO LOVE GOD WITH
OUR ALL!
THE SPIRIT OF TRUTH GUIDES IN ALL TRUTH.
SATAN IS A COUNTERFEITER.
HOLINESS IS THE SIGN OF TRUE REPENTANCE.

A HOLY PERSON SERVES GOD PASSIONATELY.
CELEBRATION CAN BE EVASIVE ACTION.
EMOTION WITHOUT ACTION IS BUBBLES.
GET CROWN, THEN CROSS.
LET GOD'S SPIRIT SIFT YOUR MOTIVES.
GOD'S GIFTS ARE NOT FOR QUARRELS.
DESPISE NOT GOD'S GIFTS.
GOD'S SPIRIT TEACHES, COMFORTS, GUIDES.
GOD'S SPIRIT EXPLAINS THE BIBLE.
THE HOLY SPIRIT IS WORTH WAITING FOR.
GOD SENDS JOY WITH HIS HOLY SPIRIT.
THE HOLY SPIRIT IS A SUPERNATURAL GIFT.
WHEN TONGUE CLANGS, APPLY LOVE.
CURE FOR ABUSE: NOT DISUSE BUT PROPER USE.
THE HOLY SPIRIT IS A SIGN OF GOD'S PRESENCE.
THE SPIRIT KNOWS HOW TO PRAY; LET HIM.
GOD'S SPIRIT HELPS EXPRESS THE INEXPRESSIBLE.
GOD' WORLD OF SPIRIT IS NOT A FAR COUNTRY.
GET EMPTIED OF SELF, FILLED WITH GOD'S SPIRIT.
TEST SPIRITUAL PHENOMENA BY THE WORD.
SATAN ALWAYS TRIES TO REWRITE THE BIBLE.
A BELIEVER CAN BE A RECEIVER.
YOU MUST BE BAPTIZED BY WATER AND SPIRIT.
POWER COMES FROM THE HOLY SPIRIT; ARE YOU WEAK?
 ASK THE HOLY SPIRIT TO HELP YOU READ THE BIBLE.
THE HOLY SPIRIT LINKS US TO JESUS.
DON'T BE TOO PROUD TO ASK FOR GOD'S SPIRIT.
THE HOLY SPIRIT IS OUR FOREMAN.
THERE IS ALWAYS SOMETHING MORE WITH GOD.
THE HOLY SPIRIT GLORIFIES JESUS.
GOOD WITNESSES NEED THE HOLY SPIRIT COUNSELOR.
THE HOLY SPIRIT IS GOD'S GIFT TO BELIEVERS.
DOES YOUR SPIRIT NEED A ROADMAP? READ THE BIBLE.
YOU KNOW GOD WHEN HE LIVES IN YOU.
THE SPIRIT WORKS IN US TO WANT TO WANT GOD'S WILL.
THE SPIRIT HELPS US OBEY GOD.
WHY RUN FROM GOD? HE BRINGS YOU GIFTS.
THE HOLY SPIRIT, NOT THE HOROSCOPE, KNOWS YOUR
    FUTURE.

GOD'S SPIRIT PURGES YOU OF DEAD WORKS.
GOD'S THREE FORMS: FATHER, SON, SPIRIT.
THE SPIRIT OF TRUTH CURES A LYING TONGUE.
THE HOLY SPIRIT IS LIKE WIND, FIRE, DOVE.
GET SAVED; GET SEALED; THEN GET BUSY.
THE HOLY SPIRIT TELLS YOU WHEN YOU SIN.
SATAN'S SWINGING TAIL IS NO MATCH FOR GOD'S SWING-
    ING SWORD.
BY GOD'S SPIRIT WE HAVE BEEN — AND ARE BEING —
    SANCTIFIED.
SPIRIT DIVINE, SANCTIFY MINE.

FORGIVENESS

ACCEPT FORGIVENESS, THEN YOU CAN FORGIVE OTHERS.
GUILT BLOCKS; FORGIVENESS FREES.
GOD FORGIVES TODAY AND FOREVER.
GUILTY? SORRY? CONFESS AND GET FORGIVEN.
FORGIVENESS: TO STEP OUT OF THE WAY SO HEAVEN CAN
    ACT.
IF YOU NEVER FORGIVE, HOPE YOU NEVER SIN.
IT'S ANNOYING TO SEE YOUR FAULTS IN OTHERS.
PASS OVER FAULTS OF OTHERS AND LOOK AT YOUR OWN.
WE ARE FORGIVEN AS WE FORGIVE.
CAN YOU FORGIVE YOURSELF?
FORGIVENESS IS A BRIDGE OVER WHICH YOU WILL NEED
    TO PASS.
FORGIVE 70 X 7.
ONCE FORGIVEN, DON'T REHEAT SINS FOR BREAKFAST.
FORGIVE YOURSELF — YOU'RE NOT GREATER THAN GOD.
YOU ARE MADE IN GOD'S IMAGE, SO YOU CAN FORGIVE.
GOD FORGIVES THE HONEST PENITENT.
A CHRISTIAN IS ONE WHO KNOWS HE'S FORGIVEN.
CLEAN YOUR HEART WITH CONFESSION AND REPENTANCE.
"FORGIVE ME" COMES FROM THE HEART, NOT FROM A
    STIFF NECK.
FORGIVENESS WARMS HEART, COOLS STING.
LOVE FAMINE? TRY EATING HUMBLE PIE.
UNFORGIVEN GUILT CAN CRIPPLE YOUR WHOLE LIFE.
THE BIBLE SAYS "THE JUDGE FORGIVES."
SOULS ARE MADE SWEET BY LOVE AND FORGIVENESS.
FAULTS ARE THICK WHERE LOVE IS THIN.

FAITH

FAITH: RESPONSE OF SOUL TO THE CALL OF GOD.
TRUE FAITH CARRIES A CROSS.
FAITH IS TRUST THAT ALL WILL WORK FOR GOOD WITH
    GOD.
FAITH GIVES UP BEING SELF-SUFFICIENT!
IF YOU HAVE FAITH, LET OTHERS LIGHT CANDLES ON IT.
CAN YOU BE INCONVENIENCED FOR YOUR FAITH?
BETTER TO WALK BY FAITH THAN BY SIGHT.
FAITH IS EXPECTANCY WORKING.
HE WHO LOSES FAITH, LOSES ALL!
IS YOUR FAITH A BEAUTIFUL PACKAGE OF NOTHING?
FAITH: BRIDGE BETWEEN MAN AND GOD!
THE POWER OF FAITH IS GREATER THAN ATOMIC BOMBS!
IS YOUR FAITH COVERED BY LAYERS OF COMPROMISES?
DON'T MISS THE JOY OF FULL FAITH.
IF YOU LACK FAITH, BORROW SOME!
FAITH GLORIFIES GOD!
FAITH CAN MAKE YOU WHOLE.
FAITH IS GIVING GOD WHAT YOU CAN'T HANDLE.
A CUT-FLOWER FAITH HAS NO ROOTS.
WHAT DO YOU SAY AT THE FUNERAL OF AN ATHEIST?
FAITH SAYS: GIVE UP BEING SELF-SUFFICIENT!
"F-A-I-T-H: FORSAKING ALL, I TAKE HIM." — PHILLIPS
    BROOKS.
FAITH AND WORKS ARE LIKE TWO OARS.
IS YOURS AN EMPTY FORM OF FAITH?
FAITH IS TRUST WITHOUT RESERVATION.
DOES YOUR FAITH HAVE WORKS?
SHALLOW LIVING CALLS FOR DEEPER FAITH.
WE CAN'T PLEASE GOD APART FROM FAITH!

LOVE

LOVE BEARS, BELIEVES, HOPES ALL THINGS.
LOVE BEGINS WITH THE PERSON CLOSEST TO YOU.
BETTER THAN TO BE LOVED IS LOVING.
THROUGH LOVE THE STRONG PROTECT THE WEAK.
GOD LOVES YOU AND WE LOVE YOU.
EVERY DAY IS PAYDAY IN LABORS OF LOVE.
LOVE SEES THROUGH A TELESCOPE — NOT A MICROSCOPE.
LOVE OFTEN RELEASES UNEXPECTED POWER.
LOVE YOUR ENEMIES — IT WILL CONFUSE THEM!
GOD'S LOVE WILL CAST OUT YOUR FEAR.
LOVE IS THE DEEPEST NEED OF OUR TIME.
WE ARE NOT CALLED TO BE SUCCESSFUL BUT TO LOVE.
LOVE YOUR NEIGHBOR AS YOURSELF.
IT'S EASIER TO LOVE THE WORLD THAN YOUR NEAREST
    RELATIVE.
THE BEST FOUR-LETTER WORD IS L O V E.
LOVE DIES WHEN WE DON'T RENEW ITS SOURCE.
HE WHO LOVES BRINGS GOD AND THE WORLD TOGETHER.
USE THINGS, BUT LOVE PEOPLE.
LOVE IS IN NO HURRY.
"LOVE ONE ANOTHER AS I HAVE LOVED YOU." — JESUS
WHY TOLERATE WHEN YOU CAN LOVE?
GOD'S LOVE IS LIKE GLUE.
HEARTS FULL OF LOVE ALWAYS HAVE SOMETHING TO GIVE.
LOVE WHAT GOD LOVES.
JESUS IS THE SOURCE OF LOVE.
LET LOVE BURN IN YOUR HEART.
WHERE THERE IS HATRED, TRY SHOWING LOVE.
IF YOU LOVE SOMEONE, YOU WILL BE LOYAL.
STUPENDOUS! GOD'S AMAZING LOVE FOR US!
"LOVE THY NEIGHBOR BUT KEEP YOUR HEDGE."
    — BEN FRANKLIN
WHAT YOU GIVE, GIVE IN LOVE.
"MAKE US INSTRUMENTS OF YOUR LOVING."
THE BEST RELIGION IS LOVE IN ACTION.
THE PUREST RELIGION IS LOVE IN ACTION.
OURS IS A CIRCLE OF LOVE.

YOU SHALL LOVE GOD WITH ALL YOUR HEART, SOUL, MIND, STRENGTH.
LOVE LOOKS FORWARD; HATE LOOKS BACK.
LOVE OR PERISH!
LOVE WHERE YOU ARE WITH THE PEOPLE THAT YOU KNOW.
GOD CREATED US WITH THE CAPACITY FOR DEEP LOVE.
IF YOU LOVE ME, LET ME SEE IT.
LOVE REQUIRES AN OBJECT.
LOVE CONQUERS HATE.
IF YOU LOVE SOMEBODY, TELL THEM!
PERFECT LOVE CASTS OUT FEAR.
BE AN ACHIEVER: LOVE NEVER FAILS.
LOVE APPRECIATES DIFFERENCES.
COMPASSION CURES MORE THAN CONDEMNATION.
LOVE IS NEVER WASTED.
LOVE IS FORGIVENESS: FORGIVENESS IS LOVE.
CULTIVATE THE ABILITY TO LOVE LIVING.
HURT PEOPLE HURT PEOPLE, BUT LOVE HEALS!
IN DEEDS OF LOVE AND MERCY THE KINGDOM COMES.
THE WAY TO ATTAIN LOVE IS BY LOVING.
NEWS: YOU CAN LOVE AND UNLOVE AT SAME TIME.
WITHOUT LOVE YOU ARE NOTHING.
GOD'S LOVE SAVES!
LOVE HELPS WITH THE HARD-TO-LIKE.
THE GREAT ALMIGHTY GOD LOVES YOU.
LEARN HOW TO LOVE GOD'S WAY.
LOVE NEIGHBOR AND ENEMY -- THEY COULD BE THE SAME.
FROM US GOD NEEDS MORE LOVE THAN PERFORMANCE.
LOVE IS FRIENDSHIP SET TO MUSIC.
LOVE IS ALWAYS A RISK, NEVER A LOSS.
GRATITUDE IS THE FRUIT OF LOVE.
A LOVING LIFE IS A FULFILLING LIFE.
A DAY IS BEAUTIFUL WHEN LOVE TOUCHES IT.
LOVE FEELINGS CAN PASS; DECISIONS TO LOVE ARE RENEWABLE.
PEOPLE AND MELONS WIN PRIZES FOR TENDER HEARTS.
LOVE, LIKE JESUS, CAN BE RESURRECTED.
LOVE CAN'T BE A ONE-WAY STREET.
FAITH IN JESUS BRINGS LOVE INTO LIFE.
JESUS LOVED. SO HE DIED — FOR YOU.

BIBLE

IF YOU WANT FLATTERY, DON'T READ THE BIBLE.
THE BIBLE THROWS LIGHT ON THE COMMENTARIES.
THE BIBLE IS GOD'S WORD TO HUMANITY.
SCRIPTURES ARE A LAMP TO GUIDE, A LIGHT FOR OUR PATH.
THE BIBLE HAS YOUR NUMBER.
O, REST IN THE LORD! WAIT PATIENTLY FOR HIM!
GOD SO LOVED THE WORLD THAT HE GAVE.
TRUST IN GOD WITH ALL YOUR HEART.
VENGENCE IS MINE — I WILL REPAY — SAYS GOD.
ASK AND YOU WILL RECEIVE.
SATAN, TOO, QUOTES SCRIPTURE!
YOUR BIBLE IS A WORK-BOOK.
THE BIBLE HELPS KEEP YOUR VALUES STRAIGHT.
"BE STILL AND KNOW THAT I AM GOD."
THE BIBLE IS A BOOK OF PSYCHOLOGY.
"PRESENT YOUR BODY AS A LIVING SACRIFICE."
IF WEEPING AT NIGHT, THEN JOY IN THE MORNING.
    PSALM 30:5
SCRIPTURE INVITES YOU TO "COME AND SEE!"
"BELOVED, LET US LOVE ONE ANOTHER."
GOD IS YOUR REFUGE AND STRENGTH!
HAVE YOU READ THE "GOOD BOOK" LATELY?
ALL WORKS TOGETHER FOR GOOD TO THOSE WHO LOVE
    GOD.
WAIT ON THE LORD AND RENEW YOUR STRENGTH!
"THE CANDLE OF THE WICKED WILL BE PUT OUT."
    PROVERBS 24:20
GOD WILL NEVER LEAVE YOU NOR FORSAKE YOU!
WHAT IS IMPOSSIBLE WITH US IS POSSIBLE WITH GOD.
THE BIBLE IS LOVE IN ACTION.
SEEK AND YOU WILL FIND, KNOCK AND IT WILL BE OPENED
    TO YOU.
THE BIBLE HELPS KEEP VALUES STRAIGHT.
THE LORD'S MY SHEPHERD — THAT'S ALL I WANT.
SATAN QUOTES SCRIPTURE BUT DODGES THE MEANING.
BE A HAPPY HEARER OF THE WORD AND OBEY IT.
STICK TO THE BOOK AND FOLLOW GOD.

YOU CAN DO ALL THINGS THROUGH CHRIST WHO
   STRENGTHENS YOU.
THE SCRIPTURES TELL OF SOMETHING MORE.
WHAT IF YOU GAIN THE WHOLE WORLD AND LOSE YOUR
   SOUL?
THE NEW TESTAMENT DESCRIBES THE HEREAFTER!
READ THE SERMON ON THE MOUNT AGAIN. MATTHEW 5-7
THE EARTH IS STILL THE LORD'S AND THE FULLNESS
   THEREOF.
GIVE THANKS TO THE LORD, FOR HIS MERCY ENDURES
   FOREVER.
LOVE ONE ANOTHER AS I HAVE LOVED YOU. JOHN 15:12
"LET THE REDEEMED SAY SO!" PSALM 107
THE BIBLE BREAKS SILENCE WITH "IN THE BEGINNING."
TRUST HIM TO HELP YOU DO IT AND HE WILL. PSALM 37:5
"FEED YOUR HUNGRY ENEMY!" PROVERBS 25:21
   GOD WILL REWARD YOU!
"DO JUSTLY, LOVE KINDNESS, AND WALK HUMBLY WITH
   GOD."
DON'T AVENGE; GOD WILL REPAY THOSE WHO DESERVE.
   ROMANS 12:19
IN ALL YOUR WAYS ACKNOWLEDGE HIM AND HE WILL
   DIRECT YOU.

SIN, SALVATION

ONCE FORGIVEN, DON'T REHEAT SINS FOR BREAKFAST.
SIN IS SEPARATION FROM GOD.
SIN IS SPIRITUAL REBELLION.
EVIL EYES SEE EVIL.
EVIL IS POWERFULLY ORGANIZED.
WE CAN SIN BY SILENCE.
INEFFECTIVE SIN: CONFESSING SINS OF OTHERS.
COMMON SIN: TO PASS BY ON THE OTHER SIDE.
MAKING SIN LEGAL DOESN'T MAKE IT RIGHT.
SIN IS THWARTING GOD'S WILL.
NEGLECT IS A SPIRITUAL TOOL OF TEMPTATION.
A REAL SINNER IS ONE WHO DOESN'T NEED GOD'S LOVE.
THE WAGES OF SIN ARE USUALLY UNREPORTED.
SIN IS REBELLION AGAINST GOD.
IF WE'RE NOT SAVED FROM SIN, WE'RE NOT SAVED FROM
    ANYTHING.
COMPLACENCY IS A SIN AGAINST THE HOLY SPIRIT.
SIN: REFUSING TO PUT YOURSELF SECOND TO GOD.
SIN IS LIVING AS IF GOD DOESN'T EXIST.
CHRIST DIDN'T FIGHT SIN BY AVOIDING SINNERS.
SIN IS THE LEPROSY OF THE SOUL.
CONFESSION IS AGREEING WITH GOD ABOUT MY SIN.
SELF-RIGHTEOUSNESS IS ONE OF THE BIGGEST SINS!
NOBODY SAID SIN WASN'T FUN!
IF WE CONFESS SIN, HE IS FAITHFUL TO FORGIVE.
CONFESSING OTHERS' SINS JUST DOESN'T DO IT!
REPENTANCE IS BEING SORRY FOR WHAT YOU'VE QUIT
    DOING.
GREATEST SIN: IGNORING GOD!
MODERN PRODIGALS SUFFER FROM "LITTLE SINS."
EASY TO SORT: SINNER, SAINT. SINNER IS THE ONE YOU
    AIN'T!
EVERY MAN HAS SOME POWER TO CHANGE HIMSELF.
ENVY WASTES TIME AND ENERGY.

WORRY, HATE, FEAR, PRIDE

MOST OF YOUR WORRIES ARE RE-RUNS!
WORRY IS UNFAITH.
WORRY IS MISUSED IMAGINATION.
DID YOU KNOW THAT WORRY IS A SIN?
WORRY KILLS LIFE.
WHY WORRY WHEN YOU CAN PRAY?
WHEN THINGS GO WRONG YOU DON'T HAVE TO GO WITH
    THEM.
WORRY IS AS USEFUL AS A PULLED TOOTH.
WORRY IS A STREAM OF FEAR IN THE MIND.
HATE IS LOVE FRUSTRATED.
HATE WILL EAT YOU UP.
HATE IS A FAILURE OF THE IMAGINATION.
LOVE IS ACCEPTING — HATE IS REJECTING.
INDIFFERENCE IS A CRUEL FORM OF HATE.
FEAR AND HATE ARE THE GRANDFATHERS OF ALL SIN.
FEAR IS SIMPLY OUR DISTRUST OF GOD.
NONE BUT THE BRAVE CAN AFFORD FEAR.
FEAR AND HOSTILITY ARE OUR DEFENSES AGAINST SEEING
    OURSELVES.
TRUST GOD AND HE WILL HELP KICK THE FEAR HABIT.
FEARS DON'T HAVE TO MASTER FAITH!
WE ARE AS CAPABLE OF HATING AS OF LOVING.
TEMPER GETS US IN TROUBLE — PRIDE KEEPS US THERE.
GOD'S PERFECT LOVE CASTS OUT FEAR.
PRIDE GOES BEFORE DESTRUCTION. Proverbs 16:8.

GENERAL

BLISS IS TO BE IN THE PRESENCE OF ONE WE TRUST
UTTERLY.
TODAY SPEAK PEACE!
APART FROM GOD YOU HAVE MANY SELVES.
BARGAIN: MY WEAKNESS FOR HIS STRENGTH.
HELL IS TO BE ETERNALLY SEPARATED FROM GOD'S LOVE.
THE ETERNAL GOD IS LOVE! RELAX!
TAKE RELAXED TIME TO RETHINK AND REORGANIZE.
EVERYONE WANTS TO BE TREATED AS A PERSON!
GOD PROTECTS THE SIMPLE-HEARTED.
YOU DIDN'T HEAR THE SUNLIGHT COME!
CALL A LONELY PERSON TODAY.
A GENERATION THAT WON'T REST A DAY IN SEVEN IS
COMING APART.
YOUTH TRIES ON FACES TO FIND ITS OWN.
DON'T DRINK TO FORGET YOU DRINK.
FLATTERY DOESN'T MATCH THE EXPECTANCY OF CONCEIT.
THE STRONG CHOOSE RIGHT AT THE RISK OF ALONENESS.
BETTER TO FORGET AND SMILE THAN TO REMEMBER AND
BE SAD.
DON'T TELL ALL YOU KNOW, BUT KNOW ALL YOU TELL.
OFTEN THERE IS A "GOOD" REASON AND THE REAL
REASON.
SYNONYM: WORD YOU USE WHEN YOU CAN'T SPELL THE
OTHER ONE.
"NOBODY'S PERFECT" CAN BE A COP-OUT.
TALENTS ARE TO BE INVESTED.
SILENCE CAN BE NOT GOLDEN BUT YELLOW.
FIT INTO CIRCUMSTANCES AND BECOME ITS VICTIM.
OLD AGE ISN'T SO BAD WHEN YOU THINK OF THE ALTERNA-
TIVE.
MOST OF YESTERDAY'S NEWS WE HAVE SURVIVED.
AWARENESS OF DEATH NEED NOT KEEP US FROM LIVING.
LIFE IS MOSTLY WALKING AND NOT FAINTING.
SOME MUDDY SHALLOW WATER TO MAKE IT LOOK DEEP.
WHEN YOU'RE THROUGH CHANGING YOU'RE THROUGH.
AMERICA IS A TUNE TO BE SUNG TOGETHER.

IN A WAY AMERICA IS A PERSON.

WHEN WE BECOME LOCKED INTO A CREED, SOMETHING DIES.

DON'T WORSHIP BEGINNINGS!

THERE ARE GOOD AND BAD FOLKS: THE GOOD SAY WHICH IS WHICH.

NEWS: WE LIVE UNDER DIVINE JUDGMENT!

CONSERVATIVE: AS IT WAS IN THE BEGINNING, IS NOW, AND EVER SHALL BE.

WHO IS THE LOCAL SPOKESMAN FOR THE HELPLESS?

THIS IS THE DAY THE LORD HAS MADE!

BLESSED ARE THE PEACEMAKERS.

LITTLE BOY: "BRING UP A CHILD AND AWAY HE GOES!"

LIFE'S NOT RESTING BUT MOVING.

LIVE AS IF THIS IS YOUR LAST DAY ON EARTH.

THINK ON THINGS OF GOOD REPORT.

A HABIT NOT RESISTED SOON BECOMES NECESSITY.

ABUSE OFTEN MASKS AS "CONSTRUCTIVE CRITICISM."

SCOFFLAW: PAYING NO ATTENTION TO RED LIGHTS.

EVERYONE HAS BOTH COWARD AND HERO IN THE SOUL.

NOT MUCH IS DONE BY "STARTING TOMORROW."

BETTER TEACH TO FISH THAN GIVE A FISH.

YOU ARE HAPPIEST INVOLVED IN A CAUSE BIGGER THAN SELF.

DISCIPLINE IS EATING ONE POTATO CHIP.

WHEN MACHINES GET TOO POWERFUL, PUT THEM ON COMMITTEES.

COUNT YOUR BLESSINGS!

BE THANKFUL WHEN YOU TOUCH BREAD.

WORDS, NOT DEEDS — LIKE GARDEN OF WEEDS.

"I'M A NOBODY" IS AN AFFRONT TO YOUR MAKER!

A SINFUL SELF SAYS, "THE ONLY REAL LIFE IS HERE."

EACH NOBLE SERVICE WAS FIRST A FRUITFUL THOUGHT.

TODAY LISTEN FOR LAUGHTER.

LONELINESS: THE PAIN OF BEING ALONE. SOLITUDE: THE GLORY.

"IF ONLY . . ." CAN BE A REAL COP-OUT!

BETTER BE A HAS-BEEN THAN A NEVER-WAS.

WOE TO PRETENDERS OF RIGHTEOUSNESS.

DO A DISAGREEABLE JOB TODAY, NOT TOMORROW.

VOLUNTEER FOR SOMETHING GOOD.

DON'T BLAME YOURSELF UNTIL ALL POSSIBILITIES ARE GONE.

THE COURAGEOUS GO FORWARD IN SPITE OF FEARS.

YOU'RE MATURING IF YOU CAN TAKE THE BLAME!

TRY SEEING THINGS THROUGH A CHILD'S EYES.

THERE ARE MORE CAR ACCIDENTS LATE THAN EARLY.

TODAY'S KIND WORDS MAY BEAR FRUIT TOMORROW.

MAKE LIFE LESS DIFFICULT FOR SOMEONE TODAY.

LIFE SHOULD BE A SERIES OF THANK-YOU'S.

PROVERB: SHORT SENTENCE BASED ON LONG EXPERIENCE.

NO ONE IS TOO GOOD TO STAY OUT, TOO BAD TO COME IN.

IT'S A LOST DAY WHEN YOU DON'T LAUGH.

ENJOY LIFE'S SMALL PLEASURES.

TRUST AND OBEY.

DON'T TODDLE IN IMMATURITY!

REST IF YOU MUST, BUT DON'T QUIT!

MEEKNESS IS NOT WEAKNESS!

WARM, PERSONAL ENEMY KEEPS YOU FREE FROM RUST.

PARENTS: DO YOU DARE TO DISCIPLINE YOUR CHILDREN?

WHAT WE CALL "FATE" IS OFTEN OUR FOOLISHNESS!

LIVING A DOUBLE LIFE GETS YOU NOWHERE TWICE AS FAST!

POWER DOESN'T CORRUPT MEN; FOOLS CORRUPT POWER.

HELL IS TO WORSHIP OURSELVES.

SOCIETY OFTEN NEEDS — BUT USUALLY REPELS — ITS REBELS.

MEN KNOW ALL ABOUT WOMEN, NOTHING ABOUT WIVES.

GETTING ON IS GETTING UP EACH TIME YOU GET DOWN.

BE READY TO LEARN EVEN IF YOU DON'T LIKE TO BE TAUGHT.

WHEN THE DEEP MIND DIRECTS, THE BODY COOPERATES!

UTTER SECURITY IS IMPOSSIBLE IN EARTHLY THINGS.

DON'T LET TRIVIALITIES BLIND YOU TO THE ETERNAL

FACE EXPRESSIONS ARE SIGNATURES OF THE YEARS.

WE ARE WHAT WE ARE AT HOME.

SPEAK THE UNIVERSAL LANGUAGE TODAY: SMILE!

ABRAHAM HAD 13 YEARS OF SILENCE!

THE TRULY GREAT ARE HUMBLE.

THE TRULY GREAT CAN BE GENTLE.

LIFE IS TO PREPARE US FOR GREATER LIFE.

DISCOVER THE NEW CONTINENT OF THE SPIRIT!

YOU DON'T HAVE TO WAIT FOR ALL LIFE'S ANSWERS TO LIVE.

DON'T LET YESTERDAY USE UP TODAY.

BE STILL AND KNOW, THEN GET UP AND GO!

LIFE IS WHAT WE ARE ALIVE TO.

WE VALUE WHAT WE'LL GET IN LINE FOR.

WANT TO BE SAVED FROM PUNISHMENT OR SAVED FROM SIN?

THAT WHICH YOU FEAR MAY WELL COME UPON YOU.

OF OUR PRISONS, ONE OF THE WORST IS LONELINESS.

THE THORNBUSH BY THE WAYSIDE IS AFLAME WITH THE GLORY OF GOD.

"BELITTLE" MEANS HE CUTS YOU DOWN TO HIS SIZE.

BIRDS FACE INTO THE WIND TO KEEP FEATHERS IN PLACE.

TO UNDERSTAND IS TO PARDON.

SOME DAY WE WILL STAND IN JUDGMENT!

MERCY MAKES ROOM FOR THE OUTCAST.

THERE IS A PRISON OF SELF-CONCERN.

BLESSED ARE THE TEACHABLE!

CONFESSION IS SOUL THERAPY.

THE FORCE BEHIND IDEAS OFTEN CORRUPTS THEM.

THE WILDEST COLTS SOMETIMES MAKE THE BEST HORSES.

THE FRUIT IS USUALLY OUT ON A LIMB.

WHEN ALL SEEMS LOST, THE FUTURE REMAINS.

"EVERBODY'S DOING IT" DOESN'T MAKE IT RIGHT.

NOTHING CHANGES WITHOUT DISTURBANCE.

NOTHING EARTHLY GOES FASTER THAN VACATION.

MEMORIAL DAY IS TO REMEMBER PEOPLE AND IDEALS!

TRUE PROGRESS MOVES QUIETLY WITHOUT NOTICE.

WRONG IS WRONG EVEN IF EVERYONE IS FOR IT!

LIES OFTEN WEAR A PLEASANT FACE.

TIME GOES SLOW WHEN YOU FAST, BUT IT'S WORTH IT.

THE WEIGHT OF TOMORROW WILL BREAK ANY BRIDGE.

COURAGE IS FEAR THAT HAS SAID ITS PRAYERS.

WHEN WE DIE WE LEAVE BEHIND WHAT WE HAVE AND TAKE WHAT WE ARE.

BETTER RISE IN LAUGHTER ABOVE LIFE THAN BEWAIL IT.

WHERE THERE'S LIFE, THERE'S HOPE.

TO ACHIEVE GOALS GET GOING — BODIES AT REST STAY AT REST!

LIQUOR IS A "SOCIALLY-ACCEPTABLE" STUMBLING BLOCK!

SHORT SERMON: GET CHANGED, GET TOGETHER, GET GOING.

CHRISTIAN PSYCHIATRY HELPS FREE PEOPLE ENOUGH TO SURRENDER TO GOD.

DO TO OTHERS WHAT YOU WANT THEM TO DO TO YOU.

SMILE: IT'S A LANGUAGE EVEN BABIES UNDERSTAND.

TO DISCOVER YOUR GOOD MEMORY, TRY TO FORGET.

THE ROAD TO HELL IS PAVED WITH GOOD INTENTIONS.

COURAGE IS NEEDED HOURLY TO CHOOSE RIGHT FROM WRONG.

GOOD JUDGEMENT COMES FROM USING BAD.

WE MUST MASTER THE TONGUE TO BE FULLY HUMAN.

THE FUTURE COMES ONE DAY AT A TIME.

IT'S WRONG TO SEE ONLY WRONG IN OTHERS.

OUR SOULS ARE RESTLESS TILL THEY REST IN GOD.

REMEMBER THE POOR — JESUS DID.

THE BROOK LOSES ITS SONG WHEN ROCKS ARE REMOVED.

SOME STAND FOR ANYTHING PEOPLE WILL FALL FOR.

ANY SOCIETY IS 25 YEARS FROM BARBARISM.

LIVE ONE DAY AT A TIME.

SOME PEOPLE ARE SLIDING TO HELL ON THEIR "BUTS."

A SMILE IS THE MAGIC LANGUAGE OF DIPLOMACY.

YOU DON'T HAVE FOREVER TO DO AS YOU LIKE!

TO BECOME STRONG, LIFT HEAVY WEIGHTS.

TODAY WE DON'T CRUCIFY — WE CLASSIFY!

SUSPICION IS MORE LIKELY TO BE WRONG THAN RIGHT.

SOME WOULD USE CATCHER'S MITT ON BOTH HANDS.

TO CURE BEING LONELY, CALL A LONELY PERSON.

LIFE DOES NOT CONSIST OF AN ABUNDANCE OF THINGS.

THE LEARNED CARRY THEIR WEALTH WITH THEM.

GARBAGE IN, GARBAGE OUT.

POLITICIANS THINK OF THE NEXT ELECTION; STATESMEN, THE NEXT GENERATION.

HALF WAY IS NO WAY.

HELD CLOSE TO THE EYE, A PENNY WILL BLOT OUT THE BIGGEST STAR.

EXPERIENCE IS SOMETHING YOU DON'T GET FOR NOTHING.

WHAT ARE YOU DOING WITH YOUR NEED TO BELONG?

CIVILIZATION HAS TO BE REBUILT IN EVERY AGE; WE'RE DOING IT DAILY.

RUDENESS IS THE "IMITATION STRENGTH" OF THE WEAK.

PATIENCE ENJOYS THE DISTANCE BETWEEN PROMISES.

GREED IS OVERCOME BY SERVICE.

LIFE IS MOST EXCITING WHEN LIVED FOR OTHERS.

THE FUTURE IS GETTING SHORTER AND SHORTER.

WALK YOUR WORRIES AWAY.

"I DON'T HAVE TIME" DOESN'T STATE FACT, BUT INTENT.

THE MATURE CAN TAKE BLAME WHICH IS NOT EVEN THEIRS.

THE MATURE CAN GRANDFATHER IDEAS — WITHOUT CREDIT.

LIVING IS CONVERSION FROM LOWER TO HIGHER FORMS.

TIME TO GET BETWEEN TOP AND BOTTOM DEPENDS ON WHICH WAY YOU'RE GOING.

SCIENCE TURNS TO RELIGION AND SAYS, "SAVE US OR WE PERISH."

UNUSED EXPERIENCE IS A DEAD LOSS.

GOOD LIFE: EARNING, LEARNING, YEARNING.

THE REAL BEDROCK OF CHRISTIANITY IS REPENTANCE.

THE ANT PREACHES BEST AND SHE SAYS NOTHING.

MARTIN LUTHER: "I WOULD HAVE PREFERRED THE PEACEFUL DAYS OF THE MONASTERY."

THE STUPID DON'T HAVE TO MAKE EXCUSES FOR MISTAKES.

MAN'S HELPLESSNESS IS GOD'S OPPORTUNITY.

HE WHO CHEATS AT PLAY WILL CHEAT ANOTHER WAY.

HE WHO SCATTERS THORNS SHOULD NOT GO BAREFOOT.

TO LEARN ONE'S BAD POINTS, PRAISE HIM TO ANOTHER.

BE INTERESTED IN THE FUTURE; YOU'LL SPEND YOUR LIFE THERE.

MEEKNESS IS POWER UNDER CONTROL.

JOGGERS MAY NOT LOSE FAT, BUT BLISTERS MAKE LOOK TALL.

SOMETIMES JUSTICE STINGS MORE THAN INJUSTICE.

BE A SPIRITUAL EXPLORER: REACH FOR SOMETHING MORE.

A CUP OF COLD WATER: ANY SPONTANEOUS ACT OF CARING.

LITTLE CAN VEX LIKE THE OPPOSITE SEX.

GET ANGRY SLOWLY; THERE'S PLENTY OF TIME.

YOU KNOW YOU BELONG WHEN YOU KNOW YOU'RE NEEDED.

TO GET A MAN DOWN YOU MUST STAY DOWN WITH HIM.

DIAMONDS: CHUNKS OF COAL THAT HUNG IN THERE!

TODAY IS THE TOMORROW YOU WORRIED ABOUT YESTERDAY.

KEEP A FAIR-SIZED CEMETERY FOR FAULTS OF FRIENDS.

THREE WAYS TO BRING UP A CHILD: EXAMPLE, EXAMPLE, EXAMPLE.

IT'S EASIER TO FIGHT FOR PRINCIPLES THAN LIVE UP TO THEM.

THE WORLD BELONGS TO THE ENTHUSIAST WHO KEEPS COOL.

TODAY IS READY CASH — USE IT.

IT'S AS MUCH A CRIME TO STARVE A BALLOT BOX AS TO STUFF IT.

INTEGRITY DOESN'T NEED RULES!

IF YOU HAVE KNOWLEDGE LET OTHERS LIGHT CANDLES AT IT.

THE MENTALLY HEALTHY CAN SAY "YES," "NO," "WHOOPPEE."

IF AMERICA DOESN'T OBEY GOD HE MIGHT GET ALONG WITHOUT IT.

WHY DOES "SWEET REVENGE" LEAVE A BITTER TASTE?

YOU CAN DO ALL THINGS THROUGH CHRIST'S STRENGTH.

WHEN WE GET TO GREENER PASTURES WE CAN'T CLIMB FENCES.

IT'S DANGEROUS TO MESS WITH THE OCCULT.

DON'T WEEP FOR THOSE LEAVING MORE IN LIFE THAN THEY TAKE OUT.

HAVE YOU BEEN CARVING IDOLS TODAY?

38

PRAYER AND PRAISE

PRAYER TEACHES WHAT TO DO.
"ASK AND YOU WILL RECEIVE!"
CAST YOUR CARE ON HIM, WHO CARES FOR YOU.
PRAYER CLEARS DUST FROM WINDOWPANES OF SOULS.
WHAT ABOUT PRAYING WHILE JOGGING?
DAILY DEVOTIONS CLEAR MIXED EMOTIONS!
PRAISE THE LORD FOR THE BEAUTY OF THE EARTH.
"HELP ME TO SAIL ON WHEN I DON'T WANT TO, LORD!"
THE FEEBLEST KNOCK OPENS HEAVEN'S DOOR!
WHEN PRAYING FOR RAIN, BRING AN UMBRELLA!
"CREATE IN ME A CLEAN HEART, O GOD!"
PRAISE THE LORD AT ALL TIMES.
NOW TRY PRAYER!
CONFESSION IS PRAYER'S PORT OF ENTRY.
LEAVE YOUR BURDEN AT OUR ALTAR.
PRAYER IS A FRESH TOUCH OF GOD.
"PRAISE" AND "REJOICE" ARE IN THE BIBLE 550 TIMES!
PRAYER CAN REALLY CHANGE YOUR LIFE!
"GOD, DON'T JUST FORGIVE US — CHANGE US!"
PRAYER IS DEEPLY FOCUSING ATTENTION **GODWARD.**
PRAYER IS AN INSIDE JOB.
PRAYER IS SOMETIMES LIKE A MIRROR.
YOUNGSTER: "I'M SAYING PRAYERS — ANYBODY WANT
    ANYTHING?"
WIPED OUT? ASK GOD FOR NEW POWER!
"THY WILL BE DONE" IS A PRAYER FOR CHANGE!
DON'T BE ANXIOUS.
CONFESSION IS LIKE EXHALING!
NEGATIVE PRAYER CAN BE AN AFFIRMATION.
KNEELING KEEPS YOU IN GOOD STANDING WITH GOD.
YOU CAN BE PRAYED FROM SICKNESS TO HEALTH.
"LORD, HELP ME TO HANG IN THERE!"
PRAYER IS OPENING YOUR LIFE TO GOD.
THE PURE IN HEART ARE THOSE PRAYED UP.
PRAY FOR THOSE WHO ARE AGAINST YOU.
MORE THAN PRAISE GOD WANTS CHRIST-LIKE LIVING.
GET A PRAYER PARTNER — IT'S GREAT!

IN PRAYER, BRING YOUR WHOLE LIFE TO GOD.
PRAYER IS OIL FOR THE DAILY GRIND.
YOU'RE NOT PRAYING TO A STATIC GOD!
PRAY FIRST, THEN PLAN.
"CONFESS YOUR FAULTS THAT YOU MAY BE HEALED."
PRAYER IS HIGHER THAN THE WILD BLUE YONDER!"
PRAYER IS PUTTING SELF UNDER GOD'S INFLUENCE.
PRACTICE WHAT YOU PRAY!
YOU ARE WHAT YOU PRAY!
IT'S OKAY TO PRAY IN CRISES!
ALL OUR SUPPLY COMES FROM GOD.
SOME PRAYERS ARE SPOILED BY OUR OWN SHADOWS.
"AND, GOD, SEND CLOTHES TO THE LADIES IN DADDY'S
    MAGAZINES."
FOR LONG-STANDING PROBLEMS, TRY KNEELING.
GOD IS ONLY A PRAYER AWAY.
THREE WORDS RESTORE TO FULL FELLOWSHIP: "I HAVE
    SINNED."
CRY TO THE LORD IN TROUBLE — HE WILL DELIVER YOU.
TAKE EVERY LITTLE THING TO GOD.
PRAYER BEGINS WHEN WE CLAIM BEING GOD'S CHILD.
GO FORWARD, AND LET GOD OPEN DOORS FOR YOU.
WHILE I LIVE, I WILL PRAISE THE LORD!
"IT'S ME, O LORD, STANDING IN NEED OF PRAYER."
TO GET THE PAST STRAIGHTENED OUT, CONFESS IT OUT!
PRAYER IS A TRUCK HEADED FOR GOD'S WAREHOUSE!
PRAYER IS THE SOUL OF RELIGION.
TAKE A MINUTE NOW TO THANK GOD.
PRAYER IS THE LINK BETWEEN THIS LIFE AND THAT TO
    COME.
IT'S A PRIVILEGE TO CARRY ALL TO GOD IN PRAYER.
IT'S HARD TO WORRY AND PRAY AT THE SAME TIME!
"PRAY EVERY NIGHT?" "NO, SOME NIGHTS I DON'T NEED
    ANYTHING!"
FASTING CLEANS OUT THE SYSTEM.
JESUS SAID, "WHEN YOU FAST..."
IF YOUR KNEES KNOCK, KNEEL ON THEM.
PRAY EASY — PRAYER DOESN'T DO IT, GOD DOES IT!
PRAYER IS DEEP CALLING TO DEEP.
BE STILL AND GIVE GOD SOME OF YOUR TIME!

SEEK FIRST THE KINGDOM AND YOUR NEEDS WILL BE MET.

INSOMNIA? GO TO SLEEP — GOD WAITS UP!

LIVE AS IF YOUR PRAYERS ARE ANSWERED!

GOD IS INTERESTED IN THE TINIEST THING!

DOES "WEAK RESIGNATION" DESCRIBE YOUR PRAYER FAITH?

PRAYER IS BOTH TALKING AND LISTENING.

"PRAY WITHOUT CEASING."

LIFE IS FRAGILE — HANDLE IT WITH PRAYER!

TO LOSE THE BURDEN OF GUILT, CONFESS IT!

PRAY — JESUS UNDERSTANDS YOU!

PRAY FOR ONE ANOTHER THAT YOU MAY BE HEALED.

IN PRAYER WE ARE BIDDEN TO TAKE EVERYTHING TO GOD.

PEOPLE NEVER OUTGROW PRAYER.

THE BEST IDEAS COME FROM HEAVEN — ON REQUEST.

"LORD, MAKE ME AN INSTRUMENT OF YOUR PEACE."

SIMPLE PRAYERS ARE OKAY — JESUS SAID "DADDY."

ARE YOU GOOD AT THE LISTENING PART OF PRAYER?

PRAYER IS THE SWORD OF SAINTS.

PRAYER IS A PRIVILEGE — TAKE IT!

PRAYER — KEY BY DAY, LOCK BY NIGHT!

AT THE ALTAR, THERE IS PEACE.

SAINTS LEARN TO SIN LESS, CONFESS MORE.

GOD WARMS HIS HANDS AT THE PRAYING HEART.

THE GREATEST THING THE GREATEST MAN EVER DID WAS PRAY.

PRAYER CHANGES THINGS — AND PEOPLE WHO CHANGE THINGS.

WITH TABLE GRACE, ALL MEALS ARE SACRAMENTS.

IN EVERYTHING GIVE THANKS.

TRY THE "PRAYER OF HELPLESSNESS."

MATURE PRAYER MOVES FROM "GIVE ME" TO "MAKE ME."

PRAY EVEN WHEN YOU DON'T FEEL LIKE IT!

PRAYER: "STAB MY SOUL FIERCELY WITH OTHERS' PAIN."

JESUS DIDN'T ARGUE THAT GOD ANSWERS PRAYERS — HE PRAYED!

PRAYER BEGINS AND ENDS WITH GOD."

LORD, FORGIVE ME FOR MEDIOCRE OBEDIENCE!

PRAY: "WHAT IS YOUR WILL IN THESE CIRCUMSTANCES?"

"LORD, SHOW ME, CLEANSE ME, USE ME."

GOD CAN HELP BEST WHEN YOU SAY, "I NEED YOU."
ASK AND YOU WILL RECEIVE, AND YOUR JOY WILL BE
    COMPLETE.
LET STOP LIGHTS BE A CALL TO PRAYER.
GOD SAYS: GIMME FIVE!
PRAY FOR OUR PRESIDENT.
PRAY FOR OUR COUNTRY.
DID YOU PRAY FOR ANYONE TODAY?

SATIRE

NEEDED: ALARM CLOCK TO HELP RISE TO THE OCCASION.
PROSPERITY MEANS GOING BROKE MORE SLOWLY.
HE WHO PROFITS FROM OTHERS' EXPERIENCES WRITES BIOGRAPHIES.
CHIVALRY — MAN DEFENDING WOMAN AGAINST ALL BUT HIMSELF.
"IF A COW GIVES MILK, IT NEED NOT PLAY THE PIANO."
ALL'S WELL THAT ENDS.
"MAYBE" IS OFTEN A FORM OF NEGATIVE THINKING.
PEOPLE WHO HAVE MOST BIRTHDAYS LIVE LONGEST.
DO YOU HAVE A MURMUR? YES, AND A PURPUR TOO.
COACH — ONE WHO WILL LAY DOWN YOUR LIFE FOR THE SCHOOL.
CYNIC: ONE WHO, SMELLING FLOWERS, LOOKS FOR A COFFIN.
OYSTER — A FISH BUILT LIKE A NUT.
SUBURBIA: THE ONLY THING IN WALKING DISTANCE IS YOUR CAR.
PSYCHOLOGY CAN LUMP ALL YOUR NAGGING LITTLE WORRIES INTO ONE BIG COMPLEX.
TO AVOID NOSE BLEED, KEEP OUT OF OTHERS' BUSINESS.
PEOPLE LIVING IN GLASS HOUSES NEED GOOD BLINDS.
IT'S EASIER TO RESTRAIN A FANATIC THAN REVIVE A CORPSE.
THE WICKED WORK HARDER FOR HELL THAN THE GOOD FOR HEAVEN!
A WORD TO THE WIFE IS SELDOM SUFFICIENT.
ROOM FOR IMPROVEMENT IS BIGGEST IN HOUSE.
ODD: FAT CHANCE AND SLIM CHANCE ARE THE SAME!
FOR A GOOD DAY AT THE RACES, DON'T GO.
DON'T GO THROUGH LIFE STANDING AT THE COMPLAINT COUNTER.
CHARITY BEGINS AT HOME BUT SHOULDN'T STAY THERE.
WOMEN'S MINDS ARE CLEANER THAN MEN'S — THEY'RE CHANGED MORE OFTEN.
SNEAKIEST WORDS: "PLUS TAX."

BORE: ONE WHO TALKS WHEN YOU WANT HIM TO LISTEN.

MORE FISH OUT OF STREAM THAN IN IT!

ANYBODY WHO CAN SWALLOW ASPIRIN AT A DRINKING FOUNTAIN DESERVES TO GET WELL.

WE PLOUGH ALONG, SAID THE FLY TO THE OX.

PRAISE: WHAT YOU GET WHEN YOU ARE NO LONGER ALIVE.

LABOR DAY: WHEN NO ONE DOES ANY.

SOME INVESTIGATORS WOULD LOOK FOR BONES IN ANIMAL CRACKERS!

BIRTHDAY: MAN GETS DAY OFF: WOMAN, YEAR.

A COMPUTER IS NEEDED TO FIGURE OUT WHAT DOESN'T ADD UP.

THOSE RUN DOWN WIND UP IN HOSPITAL.

IF THE PYRAMIDS WERE BUILT TODAY, IMAGINE THE PAPER WORK!

IN CHRISTMAS SHOPPING MANY CHARGE RIGHT AHEAD.

A SMALL JACK CAN LIFT CAR; MUCH JACK TO KEEP IT UP.

HE WHO HAS APPENDIX AND TONSILS IS DOCTOR.

BLACKSMITHS ARE USUALLY NOT GOOD AT FIXING WATCHES.

HOW CAN YOU FEEL FIT AS A FIDDLE WHEN SHAPED LIKE A CELLO?

UNEASY LIES THE HEAD THAT IGNORES A NIGHT PHONE CALL.

IF THE SHOE FITS, YOU'RE NOT ALLOWING FOR GROWTH.

GOOD-SPORT PROBLEM: HAVE TO LOSE TO PROVE IT.

A FRIEND IN NEED IS A FRIEND TO FEED.

TO DISPOSE OF HONEY, BEES CELL IT!

THE 23-HOUR DEODORANT GIVES YOU TIME FOR YOURSELF.

YOUNGER GENERATION ALIKE IN MANY DISRESPECTS.

PUNCHY AND JESTS-FOR-FUN

HORSE SENSE KEEPS HORSES FROM BETTING ON PEOPLE.

SOCRATES GAVE GOOD ADIVCE AND THEY POISONED HIM!

MEMORY IS WHAT TELLS YOU YOUR ANNIVERSARY WAS YESTERDAY.

TODAY KIDS SAY THEY CAN MAKE HISTORY FASTER THAN LEARN IT.

NOAH QUIT SAYING — INTO EVERY LIFE SOME RAIN MUST FALL."

FUN — HAVING LOTS TO DO WHEN NOT DOING IT.

THE BEST TIME TO RELAX IS WHEN YOU DON'T HAVE IT.

WHEN TWO RIDE A HORSE, ONE MUST RIDE BEHIND.

COURAGE IS NOT EQUAL PARTS OF WATER AND BOURBON.

EXPERIENCE: SOMETHING THAT ENABLES YOU TO RECOGNIZE A MISTAKE WHEN YOU MAKE IT AGAIN.

LIFE — BY THE YARD IT'S HARD — BY THE INCH IT'S A CINCH.

RETIREMENT PROBLEM: DRINKING COFFEE ON YOUR OWN TIME.

CAPITALISM — MORE DOUGH; COMMUNISM — MORE DOLE.

JUMP AT CONCLUSIONS, SCARE BEST ONES AWAY.

A TEXAN WAS SO RICH HE HAD A DENTIST FOR EACH TOOTH.

NEW SURGEON DOLL — WIND AND OPERATE ON BATTERIES.

TO GET TO BE 100 — LIVE TO 99 AND BE VERY CAREFUL.

FLEAS GOING TO DOG RACE JUST CATCH A GREYHOUND.

THE BEST ABOUT "THE GOOD OLD DAYS" (THE DAYS OF "WAY BACK WHEN") IS FRANKLY THIS RELENTLESS TRUTH: WE WERE YOUNGER THEN.

ALL I WANT FOR MY BIRTHDAY IS NOT TO BE REMINDED OF IT.

GIRL IN CAR WORTH FIVE IN PHONE BOOK.

HE WHO HESITATES IS PUSHED.

OUR HUMOR IS TOO GOOD TO BE NEW.

GOD TEACHES THROUGH LOVE — AND BURRS UNDER THE SADDLE.

REALLY, MOST MONEY IS TAINTED — TAIN'T YOURS, TAIN'T MINE.

FILTER-TIPPED MARIJUANAS WON'T DO IT.

FOURTEEN OUT OF EVERY TEN PEOPLE LIKE CHOCOLATE.

PATIENTS SHOULD NOT LEAVE HOSPITAL UNTIL STRONG ENOUGH TO FACE CASHIER.

CANNIBAL LIKED TO STOP WHERE THEY SERVED TRUCK DRIVERS.

FLEEING FROM TEMPTATION, BE SURE NOT TO LEAVE FORWARDING ADDRESS.

HE WAS SO NARROW MINDED HE COULD LOOK THROUGH A KEYHOLE WITH BOTH EYES.

LONGEST WORD — "AND NOW A WORD FROM OUR SPONSOR."

THE MORE WE LOOK AT TEMPTATION, THE BETTER IT LOOKS.

PUT OFF UNTIL TOMORROW WHAT YOU'LL BOTCH TODAY.

BACHELORS— FOUR WAYS TO KEEP HAPPY: N S E AND W.

BE CAREFUL OR YOU MAY GET WHAT YOU WANT.

BEST WAY TO MISS A TRAIN — AT A CROSSING.

A HARD INSTRUMENT TO PLAY — SECOND FIDDLE.

DOG GOES TO FLEA CIRCUS AND STEALS SHOW.

LIVE WITHIN YOUR INCOME — EVEN IF YOU HAVE TO BORROW THE MONEY TO DO IT.

OPPORTUNITY KNOCKS ONCE — TEMPTATION BANGS FOR YEARS.

SCOUTS NEVER GET DIZZY DOING GOOD TURNS.

TO MEET EXPENSES JUST TURN AROUND. THERE THEY ARE!

A DRUM IS WHAT YOU BUY FOR YOUR ENEMY'S CHILDREN.

EVEN ON THE RIGHT TRACK YOU CAN GET RUN OVER BY JUST SITTING THERE.

A KILLER SYNDROME IS BMB — BEHOLD ME BUSY.

TO GET YOUR NAME IN THE PAPER, CROSS THE STREET READING ONE.

THE COURSE OF TWO LOVES DOESN'T RUN SMOOTHLY.

ACTRESS TO DENTIST: "FIRST ROW R. IN BALCONY."

GOD GIVES THE MILK BUT NOT THE PAIL.

MARRY IN HASTE AND REPENT IN-SOLVENT.

DIFFICULT AGE HAS COME AND LIT — TOO TIRED TO WORK, TOO POOR TO QUIT.

NEW: WASH AND WEAR MINK.

THE BIGGER THE FIGGER; THE QUICKER THE SNICKER.

FIRST LIE DETECTOR FROM RIB OF MAN. IT's still the best.

IF YOU HAVE FEW FAULTS, MAKE THE MOST OF THEM.

YOU'RE A DAY CLOSER TO YOUR PENSION!

THE COMPUTER CAN NO MAN TAME.

MONEY IS OFTEN THE FRUIT OF EVIL AS WELL AS ITS ROOT.

WE SERVE BLENDED COFFEE — TODAY'S AND YESTERDAY'S.

IT IS GOOD FOR A CELLIST TO HAVE BOW LEGS.

IF ADAM RETURNED HE'D RECOGNIZE ONLY THE JOKES.

SMILES ARE LIKE SUNSHINE TO FLOWERS.

MUSTARD IS NO GOOD WITHOUT HOT DOGS!

DON'T BUY ANYTHING WITH A HANDLE ON IT. IT MEANS
WORK.

ALL'S FAIR IN LOVE AND GOLF.

EVEN IF FATE COLORS YOUR LIFE, YOU CAN CHOOSE THE
COLOR.

WE'RE ALWAYS GETTING READY TO LIVE BUT NEVER LIV-
ING

DUET: SHE PLAYS BY EAR, HE FIDDLES WITH WHISKERS.

ADVANTAGE OF THE REALLY OLD — THEY STOP CALLING
YOU OLD.

IN VIEW OF WORLD SITUATION, PLANT ANNUALS THIS
YEAR.

THE FAINT-HEARTED ARE ABDICRATS!

PSYCHIATRIST IN NUDIST CAMP IS THE ONE LISTENING.

WEAVE IT IN THIS WORLD, WEAR IT IN THE NEXT.

YOU CAN LEAD A BOY TO COLLEGE BUT YOU CAN'T MAKE
HIM THINK.

IT'S SO DRY THE WATER IS ONLY WET ON ONE SIDE.

HOTHEADS SELDOM SET THE WORLD ON FIRE.

TO LIVE NOT ON BREAD ALONE, MAKE A SANDWICH.

YOU'LL NEVER PUT FOOT IN CLOSED MOUTH.

THE HARDEST THING ABOUT SKATING IS ICE.

"TREE SURGEON FALLS OUT OF HIS PATIENT."

NEW FIRE/THEFT INSURANCE: PAYS WHEN HOUSE IS
ROBBED WHILE BURNING.

HE'S A PERSON WHO TALKS THINGS OVER AND OVER AND
OVER AND OVER . . .

ALL SOME GET ON SILVER PLATTER IS TARNISH.

A SEASICK ONE NEVER PUTS ON AIRS.

ENJOY POVERTY! YOU CAN BRAG ABOUT IT LATER.
FOOTBALL IS ONLY A GAME — NEVERTHELESS BEAT
———————.

A NARROW MIND AND A WIDE MOUTH GO TOGETHER.
STEPS TO TAKE WHEN A LION CHASES YOU: LONG ONES!
HUMILITY — WHEN YOU KNOW YOU HAVE LOST IT!
FOR SELF-SERVICE DAIRY, CROSS COW WITH OCTOPUS.
EVEN THE BUSY HAVE TIME TO TELL HOW BUSY THEY ARE.
INFLATION — WHEN THE BUCK STOPS NOWHERE!
DON'T WASTE TOO MUCH TIME TELLING HOW BUSY YOU
   ARE.
SOME THINK THEY ARE AS GOOD AS THEY NEVER WERE!
I DON'T MAKE THE SAME MISTAKE TWICE: 3 OR MORE
   TIMES USUALLY.
LAUGHTER OFTEN DECIDES THE HIGHEST MATTERS.
A PSYCHIATRIST WAS SO POPULAR, COUCH HAD UPPER AND
   LOWER BERTHS.
NEVER LET GRASS GROW UNDER YOUR FEET — IT TICKLES.
LIVE SO WHEN YOU DIE THE UNDERTAKER WILL BE SORRY!
SOCIAL SECURITY RESCUED! AT MIDNIGHT ALL AMERICANS
   TO BE TEN YEARS YOUNGER.
COMBO LEADER NAMED HIS GROUP "ELECTRIC." HE'S A
   FAN.
LIBERAL: FEET FIRMLY PLANTED IN MID AIR.
SINCE YOU CAN'T TAKE IT WITH YOU, IRS REMOVES TEMP-
   TATION.
THE WRIGHT BROTHERS LACKED A PLANE UNTIL THEY
   MADE ONE.
HE GOT IT ALL TOGETHER — BUT COULDN'T FIGURE OUT
   WHAT IT WAS.
PATIENT: "TROUBLE WITH BREATHING." DOC: "I CAN STOP
   THAT."
MANY POLITICIANS DO WORK OF TWO MEN — LAUREL AND
   HARDY.
HUMOR IS A HOLE LETTING OUT SAWDUST FROM STUFFED
   SHIRTS.
IF MAN COULD UNDERSTAND WOMEN HE STILL WOULDN'T
   BELIEVE IT.
TODAY IS THE FIRST DAY OF THE REST OF YOUR LIFE.
OLD MOVIE: COWBOY RIDING A DINOSAUR.

BE A MONKEY'S UNCLE — GIVE TO THE ZOO.

SO YOU THINK IT'S HOT HERE!

SELF-MADE MEN OFTEN WORSHIP THEIR MAKER.

IF IT GOES WITHOUT SAYING, WHY DO THEY SAY IT?

WHO SAID "TAXX" IS A FOUR-LETTER WORD?

86-YEAR-OLD GOES TO PSYCHIATRIST — MID-LIFE CRISIS.

BUMPER STICKER — "LET'S KEEP OUT OF TOUCH."

ARMY SERVE BALANCED DIET — EVERY BEAN WEIGHS THE SAME.

TO BE A STANDOUT BEAUTY, MIX WITH THE UGLY.

REMEMBER: THE RABBIT'S FOOT DIDN'T WORK FOR THE RABBIT.

DON'T LEAVE THE DOCK BEFORE YOUR SHIP COMES IN.

MONEY IS EITHER YOUR SERVANT OR YOUR MASTER.

BEST USED CAR BUY: WHEN IT'S NEW.

WE HAVE EVERYTHING CREDIT WILL BUY.

COST OF GIVING: INCOME PLUS 10%.

TO RESIGN FROM HUMAN RACE, WHERE DO YOU SEND IT?

SUNDAY IS NOT A SPONGE TO WIPE OUT THE WEEK'S SINS!

WEAPONS FOR 4TH WORLD WAR — ROCKS.

TEACHER — "EITHER I LOST A KID OR A SNOW SUIT CAME EMPTY."

WOMEN MAKE FOOLS OF MEN ONLY WITH COOPERATION.

TO HAVE CAKE AND EAT TOO, BAKE TWO CAKES.

GIVE HER AN INCH AND SHE'LL TRY TO PARK IN IT.

CONSERVATIVE: "NOTHING SHOULD BE DONE FOR THE FIRST TIME."

"EARLY BIRD GETS WORM" IS FROM BIRD'S VIEWPOINT.

MEDICAL PROGRESS: "ITCH IS NOW ALLERGY."

MEN OVER 80 SHOULD CHASE WOMEN ONLY DOWNHILL.

WE RAN HIM FOR CONGRESS — BEST WAY TO GET HIM OUT OF TOWN.

A STITCH IN TIME SAVES EMBARRASSMENT.

PUT THE TV IN YOUR GARAGE FOR YOUR OWN DRIVE-IN MOVIE.

BOOK FOR INFERIORITY COMPLEX: "LOOKING OUT FOR #2."

'THE MORE YOU BUY, THE MORE YOU HAVE TO DUST.

LIVING RIGHT IS AS EASY AS NAILING CUSTARD PIE TO THE WALL.

WATCH OUT FOR HALF-TRUTH — IT MAY BE THE WRONG HALF.

IT'S SO HOT COWS ARE GIVING EVAPORATED MILK.

IF AT FIRST YOU DON'T SUCCEED — YOU'RE ABOUT AVERAGE.

TO STOP SMOKING, CARRY WET MATCHES.

ON SOME TVS, EDU-CHANNEL IS CALLED "OFF."

SOME OPEN MOUTHS ONLY WHEN THEY HAVE NOTHING TO SAY.

YELL IN SCHOOL OF EXPERIENCE: "OUCH!"

TOAST: "MAY YOU ACHIEVE AUTOMATIC DRIVE WITHOUT BEING SHIFTLESS."

IF MAN IS LITTLE LOWER THAN THE ANGELS, THE ANGELS MUST SOMETIMES BE ASHAMED.

ARE YOU LIVING SPIRITUALLY ON THE SOUND OF YOUR OWN VOICE?

"DOCTOR, CALL HOME." "TELL MY WIFE I DON'T MAKE HOUSE CALLS."

TOO TIGHT HALOS GIVE OTHERS A HEADACHE TOO.

IT'S GOOD TO KNOW EVERYTHING YOU TELL.

FURNITURE STORE SIGN: "WE STAND BEHIND OUR BEDS."

PROBLEM WITH BUYING ON TIME — PAYING THAT WAY.

BARKING DOGS NEVER BITE — WHILE BARKING.

WE WORK DAY AND NIGHT FOR LABOR-SAVING DEVICES.

NEW PERFUME "JOGGER" MAKES YOU SMELL TIRED.

TAKE BIG WORDS BACK AND GIVE ME TWO OR THREE LITTLE ONES.

THEIR GRASS IS GREENER BECAUSE THEY TAKE BETTER CARE OF IT.

BREAD CRUMBS COST MORE THAN BREAD!

SURGEON: "AND IN CLOSING, LET ME SAY . . ."

BETTER TO BE A SECOND HUSBAND TO A WIDOW THAN THE FIRST.

FISHING IS PERPETUAL HOPE.

LAUGH, AND WRINKLES GROW IN THE RIGHT PLACES.

THOUGH WE ARE CREATED EQUAL THERE ARE STILL LONG AND SHORT FORMS.

TRYING TO MAKE A BIG SPLASH GETS YOU INTO DEEP WATER.

NURSING A GRUDGE WON'T MAKE IT BETTER.

TOO BAD COMMON SENSE ISN'T.

MOST FAT COMES FROM EATING TOO MUCH.

OFFICER TO MILITARY COMPUTER: YES, WHAT? COMPUTER: YES, SIR!

FOR THE LAST WORD SAY, "I GUESS YOU'RE RIGHT."

WHILE THE WICKED HANG TOGETHER, THE GOOD ARE SCATTERED.

BALDNESS IS NEAT.

LOSERS SENSE DEFEAT.

TODAY EVEN SHOCK-PROOF WATCHES ARE EMBARRASSED.

BUMPER STICKER: "SMILE! YOU'RE ON REAR-VIEW MIRROR."

CACTUS SANDWICH — EAT AND PICK TEETH AT SAME TIME.

THERE ARE NO RADIO DINNERS FOR THOSE WITH NO TV.

YOU CAN'T BRING THE BOSS HOME TO DINNER. SHE'S ALREADY THERE!

HARD BOILED EGGS ARE OFTEN YELLOW INSIDE.

OPPORTUNITY KNOCKS. SIN STANDS AT THE DOOR AND WINKS.

WAR DETERMINES ONLY WHO IS LEFT.

WISE MAN: ONE SMARTER THAN HE THINKS HE IS.

TODAY THERE ARE ONLY WISE VIRGINS.

HE WHO LAUGHS LAST MAY HAVE A TOOTH MISSING.

BEFORE YOU DECIDE, HEAR OTHER SIDE.

TWO BULLS ARD NOT GOOD FOR ANY ONE CHINA SHOP.

BLESSED IS HE WHO WILL BE ON THE COMMITTEE WHEN HE WANTED TO BE CHAIRMAN.

IF WE LISTENED, MAYBE HISTORY WOULD STOP REPEATING ITSELF.

LIGHTNING DOESN'T STRIKE TWICE — IT DOESN'T HAVE TO.

AERODYNAMICALLY, THE BUMBLEBEE CAN'T FLY.

AN AGREEABLE PERSON IS ONE WHO AGREES WITH ME.

FLATTERY TURNS MORE HEADS THAN ONIONS.

FOR SINGING YOUR OWN PRAISES, VOICE LESSONS ARE NOT NEEDED.

TRAVEL AND ICE CREAM BROADENS FOLKS.

SATAN IS THE FATHER OF LIES — BUT DIDN'T PATENT HIS INVENTION.

IF YOU FEEL YOU HAVE NO FAULTS, THAT'S ONE!

THE DEATH RATE AROUND HERE IS ONE TO A PERSON.

THE BEST THROW OF THE DICE IS AWAY.

GREENER GRASS PROBLEM: WHEN IT TURNS BROWN.

NEWS: "CROSSWORD ADDICT BURIED 6 DOWN, 3 ACROSS.

OLD MOVIES NEVER DIE — THEY JUST MAKE TV.

CHILDREN NOT ONLY COMFORT OLD AGE — THEY HELP YOU REACH IT FASTER.

LOOK LIKE YOUR PASSPORT PHOTO? YOU'RE NOT WELL ENOUGH TO TRAVEL!

NEW — JOGGING SHOES WITH MOTORS.

MAN FINDS TRUTH: SATAN HELPS ORGANIZE IT.

HARDEST TUMBLE IS OVER YOUR OWN BLUFF.

TO KEEP LIPSTICK FROM SMEARING EAT GARLIC.

HE WHO LAUGHS — LASTS.

INDULGE BRINGS BULGE!

FOGHORNS MAKE ALL SEEM SO SAD AND LOST!

MANY ARE CALLED BUT FEW GET UP.

BEST THING TO DO BEHIND BACK — PAT IT!

COMMUNIST: ONE WITH NO HOPE OF BEING CAPITALIST.

BECAUSE LIQUOR IS LEGAL DOESN'T MAKE IT COMPULSORY.

A PINT OF EXAMPLE IS WORTH A GALLON OF ADVICE.

CHANGE YOUR MIND OCCASIONALLY TO KEEP IT CLEAN.

LIKE FAT PIG, MISER USELESS UNTIL DEAD.

"DOGGY DIDN'T BITE BUT HE TASTED ME."

AFTER FAST RECKLESS DRIVING MAY COME SOFT SLOW MUSIC.

TEST OF GOOD MANNERS — PUTTING UP WITH BAD ONES.

WITH BEST FOOT FORWARD BE SURE TO COVER YOUR PET CORN.

HE'S SO PREJUDICED HE WOULDN'T HEAR BOTH SIDES OF A PHONOGRAPH RECORD!

HALF OF THE THINGS SAID AGAINST POLITICIANS ARE WRONG!

KID: LET'S PLAY DOCTOR. YOU OPERATE — I'LL SUE!

WHY IS COMMON SENSE SO UNCOMMON?

AS SECOND FIDDLE, YOU'RE AT LEAST IN THE ORCHESTRA.

WHEN PIANO NEEDS MOVING, DON'T JUST CARRY THE STOOL!

HUSBAND: YOU HAVE 30 POUNDS I'M NOT LEGALLY MARRIED TO!

A ONE-HOUR OPERATION TAKES YEAR TO DESCRIBE.

AGRICULTURE IS LIKE FARMING — BUT FARMING IS DOING IT.

DON'T DRINK TO DROWN SORROW — SORROW CAN SWIM!

EVERYBODY HAS ANATOMY BUT IT LOOKS BETTER ON GIRLS.

ALL WORK AND NO PLAY MAKES JACK.

200 YEARS AGO WE WENT TO WAR TO AVOID TAXATION.

GO TO THE POOL AND SEE WHO'S COOKING.

IF A SMILE'S YOUR UMBRELLA, YOU'LL GET A MOUTHFUL OF RAIN.

IF IT WEREN'T FOR FRIENDS, YOU'D BE A TOTAL STRANGER.

YOU SHOULD BE ON THE STAGE! ONE LEAVES IN HALF AN HOUR.

CHILD: CREATURE HALFWAY BETWEEN ADULT AND TV SET.

WHAT SHE LIKES ABOUT HER HUSBAND IS HIS WIFE.

A PLACE IN THE SUN CALLS FOR SOME BLISTERS.

LATE TO BED AND EARLY TO RISE MAKES YOU BAGGY UNDER YOUR EYES.

MOSES LEANED ON HIS STAFF AND DIED.

HYPOCRITE: ONE WHO ISN'T HIMSELF ON SUNDAYS.

ZOO: WHERE ANIMALS STUDY HABITS OF HUMANS.

SHE WAS BORN IN THE YEAR OF OUR LORD ONLY KNOWS.

"DID SHE TELL HER AGE?" "PARTLY."

TEARS — REMORSE CODE.

TO KNOW HOW BAD YOU ARE, TRY TO BE GOOD.

TAKE THE BULL BY THE TAIL AND LOOK THE SITUATION IN THE FACE.

MEN SUBSCRIBED TO DOMINATION OVER WOMEN UNTIL WOMEN CANCELED THE SUBSCRIPTION.

THE TWO FORMS OF GOVERNMENT: LONG FORM AND SHORT FORM.

TO MAKE IT RAIN, WATER YOUR LAWN.

THE EARLY HUSBAND GETTETH HIS OWN BREAKFAST.

HUMILITY: WHEN YOU KNOW YOU HAVE IT, YOU DON'T.

OLD PICKPOCKETS NEVER DIE. THEY JUST STEAL AWAY.

BLACKBERRIES ARE RED WHEN THEY ARE GREEN.

"LET'S GET ANOTHER MEDICAL OPINION. LET'S CALL A DOCTOR."

WALLS OF MOTEL THIN. ASKED WIFE QUESTION, GOT FOUR DIFFERENT ANSWERS.

GIVE THE DEVIL HIS DUE, BUT DON'T LET MUCH BE DUE HIM.

HE'S OFTEN WRONG BUT NEVER IN DOUBT!

"LIVED HERE ALL YOUR LIFE?" "NOT YET."

LAST TWO WORDS OF NATIONAL ANTHEM: PLAY BALL.

BE KIND TO DUMB PEOPLE SO THAT THEY MAY BE KIND TO YOU.

THE HEAD GROWS BALD, HAIR BY HAIR!

THE MOVIE WAS SO OLD THE GIRL SAID "NO."

IF PRAYERS WERE PUDDINGS, WOULD YOU EAT WELL?

THE LATEST THING IN MEN'S CLOTHING IS WOMEN.

DISTANT RELATIVES ARE THE BEST KIND.

YOU'RE OLD WHEN ALL NUMBERS IN YOUR BLACK BOOK ARE DOCTORS.

TO KEEP STAMPS FROM STICKING TOGETHER BUY ONE AT A TIME.

DIETS HELP YOU GAIN WEIGHT MORE SLOWLY.

IF OUTGO EXCEEDS INCOME, UPKEEP IS YOUR DOWNFALL.

FREE LOVE COSTS THE MOST.

THE HARD-BOILED ARE OFTEN SOFT-BAKED.

ONE THING ABOUT LIFE — IT'S TEMPORARY.

IF YOU CAN DREAM IT YOU CAN DO IT.

TEXAS IS A STATE OF MIND.

SURE WAY TO CATCH A BUS: MISS THE ONE BEFORE.

YOU LOOK LIKE A MILLION — $124,000 AFTER TAXES.

EMBARRASSMENT: TWO EYES MEETING AT THE SAME KEY-HOLE.

TO MAKE FIRE WITH TWO STICKS — MAKE ONE A MATCH.

TYCOON TO PSYCHIATRIST: "I HATE MY PARENT COM-PANIES."

SOME PAY COMPLIMENTS EXPECTING RECEIPTS.

IN TEXAS IT WAS SO HOT THE SUN CAME DOWN AND GOT UNDER A CACTUS.

TRY MAKING ONLY NEW MISTAKES.

IT'S HARD TO PULL YOURSELF OUT OF TROUBLE WITH CORKSCREW.

WHATEVER YOU BUY TODAY IS ON SALE TOMORROW.

LIFE'S QUESTIONS DON'T BOTHER — IT'S THE ANSWERS.

REBELLING GENIE — "YOU RUB ME THE WRONG WAY."

FEW LEARN THE BUSINESS FROM THE TOP DOWN.

THE UNDERPRIVILEGED HAVE NO REMOTE CONTROL ON COLOR TV.

THE WORLD OWES YOU NO LIVING — IT WAS HERE FIRST.

A HOBBY IS GETTING EXHAUSTED ON YOUR OWN TIME.

UTILITY POLES HIT CARS ONLY IN SELF-DEFENSE.

BEST THING TO DO FOR SPRING FEVER: ABSOLUTELY NOTHING.

EVERY QUITTING TIME THERE ARE REINCARNATIONS.

BOYS WILL BE BOYS — SO WILL MANY MIDDLE-AGED MEN!

INAPPROPRIATE BEFORE SERMON: "NOW I LAY ME DOWN TO SLEEP."

IF YOU OWN LAND, CHANCES ARE IT OWNS YOU.

WHEN YOU FEEL UTTERLY HELPLESS, YOU ARE!

NO ONE NEEDS A VACATION SO BADLY AS THOSE WHO JUST HAD ONE.

TO AVOID BURNING HAND IN HOT WATER — FEEL FIRST.

MANY WILL NEGLECT AFFAIRS TO TELL YOU HOW TO RUN YOURS.

AFTER INHERITING THE EARTH, THE MEEK DON'T STAY THAT WAY.

POOR ADAM AND EVE HAD NO ONE TO TALK ABOUT.

NO WIFE EVER SHOT HER HUSBAND WHILE HE WAS DOING DISHES.

WHEN YOU'VE SEEN ONE ATOMIC WAR YOU'VE SEEN THEM ALL.

"MOST GENIUSES ARE CONCEITED — BUT I'M NOT."

LIFE IS TOO SHORT TO BE SMALL.

IN REMEMBERING, THE FUN IS THE REARRANGING.

BEEFING TOO MUCH PUTS YOU IN THE STEW.

HUMANITY IS DANDRUFF ON THE SHOULDER OF THE WORLD.

URIAH HEEPS DON'T GET CRUCIFIED.

WORRIED ABOUT LOSING MEMORY? FORGET IT!

IT'S EASIER TO BE CRITICAL THAN CORRECT.

GIVE SOME AN INCH AND THEY'LL MEASURE IT.

TYRANTS BELIEVE IN FREEDOM — FOR THEMSELVES.

MOST EXPENSIVE PER MILE: SHOPPING CART!

BELIEVING IN EVERYTHING A LITTLE BIT DOESN'T DO IT!

SOME SMOKE-FILLED ROOMS HAVE BETTER AIR THAN OUT-SIDE.

LIFE EXPECTANCY IS GREATER — NOW YOU CAN EXPECT ANYTHING.

MOST STUMBLING IS OVER MOLEHILLS!

GOOD THING ABOUT BEING POOR — IT'S INEXPENSIVE.

A FRIEND IN NEED IS A DRAIN ON THE WALLET.

HONKING IS FOR GEESE.

HOLLYWOOD: A RETAKE.

WE MIGHT KEEP UP WITH THE JONESES IF THEY WOULD MAKE PIT STOPS.

EARLY MOVIES SILENT: THEN SOUND: NOW SMELL.

THE BEST LEADER IS ONE WHO MAKES CREATIVE MISTAKES.

TO GET ALL TO READ, WRITE STRICTLY CONFIDENTIAL.

EGOTIST: PERSON OF LOW TASTE MORE INTERESTED IN HIMSELF THAN ME!

TO CURE INSOMNIA, GET LOTS OF SLEEP.

AT REUNIONS YOU SHAKE HANDS WITH MANY OLD FACES.

IF THE WORLD IS GETTING SMALLER WHY RAISE POSTAL RATES?

THE MAN WHO DISCOVERED AN AMNESIA CURE FORGOT WHAT IT WAS.

COLLEGE TEACHING: CASTING IMITATION PEARLS BEFORE REAL SWINE.

LETTER TO ALUMNI: DEAR ATHLETIC SUPPORTER.

THERE IS NOW IMITATION INSURANCE FOR IMITATION FIREPLACES.

SOUP SHOULD BE SEEN AND NOT HEARD.

THINK OF ALL THE THINGS YOU DON'T GET THAT YOU DON'T WANT!

COPS: TO DISPERSE CROWDS, TAKE AN OFFERING.

TO ERR IS HUMAN; TO BLAME IT ON OTHERS IS POLITICS.

MONEY DOESN'T MAKE FOOLS — IT JUST SHOWS THEM UP.

"AND NOW NEWS WILL BE FOLLOWED BY A MOMENT OF TRUTH."

THERE WILL BE NO WEDDING PRESENTS IN HEAVEN.

TO COOK A GOURMET MEAL: FIRST TAKE TWO CREDIT CARDS . . .

IF YOU DON'T SAY ANYTHING, YOU WON'T HAVE TO REPEAT IT.

SOME HAVE NO RESPECT FOR AGE UNTIL IT'S BOTTLED.

IF YOU DRINK TO FORGET IT — FORGET IT.

HASH IS OUT. RECYCLED LEFTOVERS ARE IN.

SPEAK SOFTLY AND CARRY A BIG STICK — OF CANDY.

DON'T MAKE A BIG GARDEN IF YOUR WIFE TIRES EASILY.

BAD TASTE IS BETTER THAN NONE AT ALL!

ANSWER MY PRAYER — STEAL THIS CAR!

NOBODY WHO CAN READ CAN CLEAN OUT AN ATTIC.

SCOUTING REMEMBRANCE: "TODAY'S BROWNIE IS TOMORROW'S COOKIE."

A FAVORITE SEAFOOD NOW IS SALT WATER TAFFY.

INVENTION IS THE MOTHER OF NECESSITY.

THE HORN OF PLENTY IS THE ONE BEHIND YOU IN TRAFFIC.

LIFE IS NOT A STATE BUT A MOVEMENT.

PENICILLIN SIGN: "TO SAVE TIME PLEASE BACK INTO OFFICE."

YOU JUST CAN'T SMUGGLE DAYLIGHT PAST A ROOSTER.

CONTROVERSY — COLLISION OF TWO TRAINS OF THOUGHT.

WHAT DO DEMOCRATS AND REPUBLICANS HAVE IN COMMON? OUR MONEY!

TO FEEL YOUR HOME IS YOUR CASTLE, GET A PAINTING ESTIMATE.

AFTER YOU CLIMB HIGH ON LADDER FRIENDS BEGIN TO SHAKE IT.

DO OPEN MOUTH WHEN CHANGING FEET.

IN THE MOVIES ILLUSION IS CREATED BY A SERIES OF JERKS.

CHILDREN ARE SPOILED BECAUSE YOU CAN'T SPANK TWO GRANDMOTHERS.

NEW COLLEGE STUDENTS ARE NOW CALLED FRESHPERSONS.

FOR EXERCISE: READ MYSTERIES AND LET FLESH CREEP.

THOU SHALT NOT STEAL.

YOU CAN GO TO HEAVEN AND SMOKE, EVEN AHEAD OF TIME!

CLEVERLY SELF-CENTERED IS STILL SELF-CENTERED.

THE MEEK SHALL INHERIT THE EARTH — LESS TAX.

ACTUAL MINUTES OF MEETING — "THE LORD'S PRAYER WAS READ AND APPROVED."

IF YOU KNOW ALL THE ANSWERS, MAYBE YOU DIDN'T UNDERSTAND THE QUESTION.

Q: GIVEN A MILLION DOLLARS, WHAT WOULD YOU BUY? A: A THANK YOU CARD.

THOSE WHO SHOOT OVER HEADS OF PEOPLE MAY NOT BE SUPERIOR — JUST POOR SHOTS.

THE GREATEST FAULT IS TO BE CONSCIOUS OF NONE.

CARELESS WOMEN LOSE GLOVES — CAREFUL ONES, ONE.

SOME HAVE NO PREJUDICE — THEY HATE EVERYONE.

AFRICAN WORD FOR MOTORCYCLE: MUDUDU.

FALL IN LOVE WITH YOURSELF AND HAVE NO RIVALS.

ETIQUETTE IS YAWNING WITH MOUTH CLOSED.

TOUGH: STAND UP TO BE COUNTED AND HAVE THEM STOP COUNTING.

IF SOME SAID WHAT THEY THOUGHT THEY'D BE SPEECHLESS.

IRONY: GIVING FATHER BILLFOLD FOR CHRISTMAS.

MOTORISTS: BETTER BE LATE THAN "THE LATE."

A SHORT VACATION IS HALF A LOAF.

PETS NEED THE STIMULUS OF FLEAS.

THOSE BURNING CANDLE AT BOTH ENDS MAY BE TRYING TO READ THE MENU.

BETTER NOT LIVE ON YOUR INTELLECTUAL FAT.

SPECIAL ENTHUSIASM IS OFTEN RESERVED FOR THE UNIMPORTANT.

IF YOU TIE WHEN RACING TRAIN TO CROSSING, YOU LOSE!

GOLF IS NOT JUST FOR RICH. THERE ARE MANY POOR PLAYERS.

IN SMELLS, FRYING BACON BEATS ORANGE BLOSSOMS.

IN ONE DAY MOTHERS MAKE MORE DECISIONS THAN THE SUPREME COURT IN THREE YEARS!

DON'T COUNT RIBS IN ANATOMY EXAMS.

THE HUMAN BODY CAN LAST A LIFETIME.

WHEN YOUR MIND LOSES THE PICTURE, TURN OFF THE SOUND.

ONE THING MONEY CAN'T BUY — POVERTY.

CARELESS FLATTERY EXHAUSTS YOU IN AN EFFORT TO BELIEVE IT.

IT'S A POOR MEMORY THAT WORKS BACKWARD.

THE HOME MOVIE VILLAIN IS THE ONE RUNNING THE PROJECTOR.

ALL MEN WILL SERVE ON THE JURY FOR A BATHING BEAUTY CONTEST.

CALL A SPADE A SPADE WHEN YOU TRIP OVER ONE!

TODAY'S PRESIDENT IS TOMORROW'S 20 CENT STAMP.

IT'S HARD TO SEE THE PICTURE WHEN YOU'RE IN THE FRAME.

"MACHO DOESN'T PROVE MUCHO." — ZSA ZSA GABOR.

THE THINNER THE ICE THE MORE SOME WILL TEST IT.

FOR CREATIVE IDEAS, TRY WALKING.

THERE'S ALWAYS ROOM AT THE TOP — AFTER THE INVESTI-
GATION.

SLEEP NEEDED BY AVERAGE PERSON: TEN MINUTES MORE.

SOME WHO LIVE ALONE LIKE IT. MANY LOOK IT!

WHAT DOES THE WORK OF TEN MEN? FIVE WOMEN!

PUNS

APATHY IS VIGOR MORTIS.
NIGHT CLUBS TAKE A DIM VIEW OF LIFE.
TROUBLE WITH LIPSTICK — IT DOESN'T!
NUDIST SIGN: "CLOTHED FOR THE WINTER."
ORTHOPEDISTS GET ALL THE BREAKS.
FOR COLORFUL SKIING — WHITE SNOW AND BLUE CROSS.
EUROPEAN TRAVEL IS FAIR TO MEDIEVAL.
THOSE WEARING SHORT-SLEEVED SHIRTS CAN'T MAKE OFF-
    THE-CUFF REMARKS.
A DENTIST GIVES KIDS A PLAQUE PLAQUE.
COAL DEALERS DO BUSINESS ON A LARGE SCALE.
A DENTIST QUIT — COULDN'T STAND THE GRIND!
EASY TO MILK COWS — ANY JERK CAN DO IT!
KNIGHTS IN MIDDLE AGES LED A DUEL LIFE.
THOSE WHO RACE TRAINS TO THE CROSSING FLY TO PIECES.
A SMILE ADDS TO YOUR FACE VALUE.
DOCTORS HIT KNEES WITH RUBBER HAMMERS FOR KICKS.
BAGDAD — WHAT MOM SAID SHE DID WHEN SHE MET HIM!
THE CLOSED MOUTH CATCHES NO FLIES.
AS THE MOLECULE SAID, "UP AND ATOM!"
SOME LIVE ALONE, BUT WOULD RATHER KNOT.
FLIRTING WITH BUTCHER IS PLAYING FOR BIGGER STEAKS.
BEAR WENT OVER MOUNTAIN TO SEE WHAT WAS BRUIN.
OVEREATING BRINGS INTERIORITY COMPLEX!
WHEN PLAYING GOLF AFTER DARK, USE NIGHT CLUBS.
AFTER-DINNER SPEAKERS START THE BULL ROLLING.
CITIES ARE CALLED "SHE" BECAUSE OF OUTSKIRTS.
OUR ROLLS RISE IN YEAST, SET IN VEST.
A BIG SHOT IS OFTEN A BIG BORE.
USED CARS ARE FINE AS FAR AS THEY GO.
DIETS ARE FOR THOSE THICK AND TIRED OF IT.
CREMATION IS SOMETHING URNED.
COW AT MILKING: "THE YANKS ARE COMING."
SHOPLIFTERS ARE SMART — PICK UP THINGS FAST.
BLACK EYES COME FROM GUIDED MUSCLES.
SOME ARE KNOWN BY DEEDS, OTHERS BY MORTGAGES.
NEW MOVIE OF LOCH NESS MONSTER AND JAWS: LOCH
    JAWS!

WITH SQUEAKY SHOES, YOU HAVE MUSIC IN YOUR SOLES.
TODAY EVEN LOW-HEELED SHOES ARE HIGH!
IN AMERICA, OBESITY IS REALLY WIDESPREAD.
MAN WHO MAKES YOU TREMBLE IN EVERY FIBRE — DEN-
TIST!
DIETERS — DON'T LET THE GOBBLINGS GET YOU!
COUNTERFEITERS RUN AFTER-DINNER MINTS!
AUCTION — WHERE YOU GET SOMETHING FOR NODDING!
A HAIR ON THE HEAD IS WORTH TWO IN THE BRUSH!
PSYCHO-COLA IS FOR THOSE WHO THINK JUNG!
**TAKE VACATION WHEN YOU CAN'T TAKE WHAT YOU'VE
BEEN TAKING.**
THE MEEK SHALL INHERIT THE WORK!
HE WHO WEARS HAIR TONIC GETS UP OILY!
ONE SNAKE TO ANOTHER: "BOAS WILL BOAS!"
TO COIN A PHRASE, "A PENNY SAVED IS A PENNY EARNED."
FOR A RUN-DOWN FEELING, TRY JAY-WALKING!
SARCASM — GETTING EDGE IN, WORD-WISE!
LARGEST FISH — PIANO TUNA!
**CAB DRIVERS ENJOY WORK: IT'S THE PEOPLE THEY RUN
INTO.**
IF YOUR HAIR IS GRAY, IT'S TIME TO DYE.
**NEW REMEDY — HALF ASPIRIN, HALF GLUE — FOR SPLIT-
TING HEADACHES.**
THE STUDY OF IMMORTALITY IS A LONG-TERM PROJECT.
ODD: BOTTLENECK IS ALWAYS AT THE TOP.
EVERYTHING COMES TO HIM WHO ORDERS HASH.
DOCTORS GET UNSOLICITED ORGAN RECITALS.
CLAM DIGGERS ARE MUSSEL-BOUND!
COURT — WHERE THEY SOMETIMES DISPENSE WITH JUS-
TICE.
REPARTEE — STRIKING WHEN THE IRONY IS HOT.
JOKER DENTIST LOST CUSTOMERS — PULLED TOO MANY
GOOD ONES.
IF TOO FAT, GET THINNER AT PAINT STORE.
"VIRUS" — MEDICAL TERM: "YOUR GUESS AS GOOD AS
MINE."
RESPONSE TO EDITORIAL: EQUAL FOR AND AGHAST.
SNACK — PAUSE THAT REFLESHES.
DERMATOLOGISTS GIVE RASH JUDGMENTS.

HOSPITAL — WHERE YOU'RE ON PINS AND NEEDLES.
THE BRAIN IS NO STRONGER THAN ITS WEAKEST THINK.
FOR PIN MONEY GO INTO ACUPUNCTURE.
YOU CAN'T KEEP HOME CIRCLE SQUARE WITH TRIANGLE.
IMITATION SPAGHETTI IS CALLED "IMPASTA."
**WITH ERECTOR SET BEVERLY HILLS KID BUILDS TAX
    SHELTER.**
ESKIMOS KEEP MONEY IN SNOW BANKS.
NO DOUBT, WOMEN ARE HERE TO SAY.
CONSCIENCE — FAULTS ALARM.
HOSPITAL TRIP — VACATION WITH PAIN.
"POOR SPELLERS OF THE WORLD — UNTIE!"
GAMBLING RENT MONEY IS A MOVING EXPERIENCE.
RAIN FALLS, BUT GETS UP IN DEW TIME.
IN TELLING AGE, WOMEN ARE SOMETIMES SHY.
THE NEW CARPENTERS' BRASS QUARTET: THE TUBA FOURS.
SEASICK SONG — "HANG YOUR HEAD OVER, LET EVERY-
    THING GO!"
WHERE DOES GENERAL KEEP ARMIES? IN HIS SLEEVIES!
SANDWICH SPREAD IS FROM EATING BETWEEN MEALS.
TV MOTTO: "TRITE MAKES RIGHT."
LEFT-HANDERS HAVE RIGHTS TOO!
A FUTURE FARMER IS AN OVERALL PERSON.
BETTER TO HAVE LOAFED AND LOST THAN NEVER TO HAVE
    LOAFED AT ALL! — THURBER
LACK OF DIETING SHAPES OUR ENDS.
THE SEASICK WOULD LIKE TO OVERRULE THE MOTION.
A RELATIONSHIP WITH YOU FIRST WON'T LAST.
CANNIBAL BOOK: "THOUSAND WAYS TO SERVE FELLOW
    MAN."
DON'T LOSE SLEEP BUYING ON THE "LAY-AWAKE PLAN."
MANY HAVE SOCIAL CIRCLES UNDER EYES.
BE CONTENT WITH YOUR LOT, IF A CORNER ONE!
WHEN DIETING, REMEMBER FIRST TO FORGET SECONDS!
TAXPAYERS ARE ALIVE AND KICKING.
HE WITH COW AND DUCKS HAS MILK AND QUACKERS.
SHE CALLED HER HUSBAND, "HENRY" — HE'S THE EIGHTH!
WHAT IF YOU STICK YOUR HEAD IN OVEN? BAKED BEAN!
IN WASHINGTON'S DAY, WHERE DID SNUFF GO? NO ONE
    NOSE!

FOR A SHORT WINTER, HAVE A NOTE DUE IN SPRING!

CONCEIT — I STRAIN.

YOU CAN GET DRUNK ON A SIP OF AUTHORITY.

CROSS LOCOMOTIVE WITH AUTO AND GET A FUNERAL.

THE ZIPPER WAS INVENTED BY MESHING AROUND.

IN DAIRYING IT TAKES PULL TO GET AHEAD.

NOAH, BAORDING ARK: "NOW I HERD EVERYTHING!"

DAIRY OWNERS OWE THEIR LIVING TO UDDERS.

CAIN WAS THE FIRST BASE MAN.

FOR REFRESHMENT, SOME SERVE A GLASS OF WHINE.

TODAY'S SONG: "I DREAM OF HARRY WITH THE LIGHT BLUE JEANS."

SHE BOUGHT A LOT IN RENO AS GROUNDS FOR DIVORCE.

PSYCHIATRISTS HAVE COUCHES FOR THOSE OFF THEIR ROCKERS.

NOTHING RECEDES LIKE SUCCESS.

TO ENTER CEMETERY AT NIGHT, USE SKELETON KEY.

ENGLAND HAS NOT ONLY A BLOOD BANK BUT A LIVERPOOL!

GIRLS, BE CAREFUL OF THE BOYOLOGICAL URGE!

HE WHO BLOWS FUSE USUALLY IN DARK.

IF AT FIRST YOU DON'T SUCCEED, DIET DIET AGAIN!

OPTOMETRISTS WHO BACK INTO LENS GRINDERS MAKE SPECTACLES OF SELVES.

ADAM AND EVE ORIGINATED THE LOOSE-LEAF SYSTEM.

TO "HERR" IS GERMAN . . .

WE'RE NEVER TOO OLD TO YEARN!

NEW GAME FOR MONOTONES: "MAIM THAT TUNE!"

A CANTALOUPE-EATING DOG: A MELON-COLLIE.

NEW SPEECH COURSE: BEGINNING FINNISH.

A HARD-BOILED EGG IS HARD TO BEAT!

ALCOHOLICS CAN BECOME TEA-TOTALERS!

AN ONION A DAY KEEPS THE DOCTOR AWAY.

A WATCHED POT OFTEN JOINS WEIGHT WATCHERS!

KID WHO SWALLOWED BUS TICKET HAD TO GET SECOND HELPING.

YARD SALE — TOO GOOD TO BE THREW!

ROBINSON CRUSOE — ONLY ONE GETTING WORK DONE BY FRIDAY.

A BIRD IN THE HAND IS POOR TABLE MANNERS!

DON'T BE WEAKENED BY TOO MUCH WEEK-END!

SLEEPER DURING POLITICAL SPEECH — BULLDOZER!

HAIRPIECE AT $200 — TOO MUCH TOUPEE!

GAFFITI IS WIT AND RUN.

THE NEUROTIC IS SELF-TAUT.

EAT, DRINK AND BE MERRY — TOMORROW YOU DIET!

SHE WANTED TO BE BUBBLE DANCER, BUT DAD SAID, "NO SOAP!"

GREATEST LABOR SAVER OF TODAY — TOMORROW!

IF YOU DON'T WATCH DIET, ALL MAY GO TO POT.

GIRLS: A RING ON THE HAND IS WORTH TWO IN THE VOICE!

A WISE MAN DOESN'T BLOW HIS KNOWS!

SIGN: "PLAIN CAKE 66¢; UPSIDE DOWN 99¢"

THE OVERWEIGHT ARE LIVING BEYOND THEIR SEAMS.

TO SPEED IS HUMAN; TO GET CAUGHT, DE FINE!

WORSE THAN RAINING CATS AND DOGS — HAILING TAXIS!

FISH IS BRAIN FOOD — ALSO NOODLE SOUP!

CONTENTMENT IS THE SMOTHER OF INVENTION.

A MILLIONAIRE IS A BILLIONAIRE AFTER TAXES.

ELEPHANTS ARE TIRED OF WORKING FOR PEANUTS.

FOR THE IDLE RICH, THE CEMETERY IS THE LAST RESORT.

TO MAKE HOT DOG STAND, STEAL ITS CHAIR.

CAN YOU BE TOP BANANA AND KEEP IN TOUCH WITH THE BUNCH?

DIPPING BREAD IN GRAVY IS IN SUCH GOOD TASTE!

THERE'S A NEW COMBINED TOOTHPASTE/SHOE POLISH FOR THOSE WHO PUT FEET IN MOUTH.

WHILE HE HAS NOT BEEN IN A PLAY, HIS LEG HAS BEEN IN A CAST!

DIETERS EAT CURDS AND WEIGH.

QUESTIONS

IS YOURS A LIFE THAT REALLY MATTERS?
CAN YOU BE A CHRISTIAN BY YOURSELF?
ARE YOU LETTING GOD LOVE YOU?
ARE YOU LETTING GOD LOVE THROUGH YOU?
DRIFTING OR ROWING?
LIVING RIGHT?
WHAT ABOUT GIVING GOD THE CREDIT?
WHO IS MORE HELPLESS THAN THE OWNER OF A SICK
   GOLDFISH?
HOW MANY PEOPLE ARE IN YOUR JAIL?
AS A NATION, WHAT DO WE REALLY HOLD DEAR NOW?
WHEN THE ROLL IS CALLED UP YONDER, WILL YOU BE
   THERE?
NOT "WHO ARE YOU?" BUT "WHOSE ARE YOU?"
DO YOU REALIZE YOU'VE NEVER LIVED THIS DAY BEFORE?
HOW ARE YOU SPENDING YOUR INFLUENCE?
HAVE YOU FORGOTTEN HOW TO BE SORRY?
ARE POSSESSIONS POSSESSING YOU?
WHEN TALKING TO SELF, EVER SNARL?
ARE YOU "VIOLENTLY GUARDING SOFT SPOTS?"
IF GOD ACCEPTS YOU, WHY CAN'T YOU ACCEPT YOURSELF?
ANY MESSAGES FROM HEAVEN LATELY?
IS GOD SHOWING YOU THAT YOU'RE PHONY?
IN SUPPORT, WHOSE HAND DO YOU HOLD THESE DAYS?
IN GOD WE TRUST?
DO YOU DARE PREACH WHAT YOU PRACTICE?
ARE YOU "TODDLING ALONG IN IMMATURITY?"
ARE YOU REALLY HONEST WITH YOURSELF?
IN 100-YEAR TERMS, WHAT IS SUCCESS?
FAITH CAN MOVE MOUNTAINS — AND YOU!
IS IT WELL WITH YOUR SOUL?
WHAT ARE YOU LIVING FOR?
ARE YOU TOO BUSY TO CARE?
WILL YOU PUT YOURSELF WHERE YOUR MOUTH IS?
DOES GOD GET FROM YOU ONLY A BUSY SIGNAL?
HOW DO YOU FEEL ABOUT RAIN ON THE JUST AND UNJUST?

CAN A MAN MARRY HIS WIDOW'S NIECE?

WHAT WOULD YOU ATTEMPT IF YOU COULDN'T FAIL?

WHAT GOOD IS A NEST EGG IF YOU ONLY SIT ON IT?

DO YOU HAVE JUST ENOUGH CHRISTIANITY FOR DISCOM-
FORT?

ARE YOU A SECRET SERVICE CHRISTIAN?

IF REACH DOESN'T EXCEED GRASP, WHAT'S HEAVEN FOR?

ARE YOU READY TO BE OFFERED?

DO YOU LIVE LIKE JESUS DIED FOR YOU?

IF YOU DON'T PAY ALIMONY, COULD YOU BE REPOSSESSED?

WHAT IS TWO-UM AND TWO-UM? FORUM!

IF YOU PLAY PIANO BY EAR, WHAT ABOUT EARRINGS?

IF YOU CHANGED YOUR NAME, WHAT WOULD YOU CALL
YOURSELF?

ARE YOU DOING YOUR HIGHEST DREAMS?

WHAT CHRIST IS KNOWN THROUGH YOU?

WERE YOU EVER BORED AT A COMPLIMENT?

WHO THINKS YOU'RE WONDERFUL?

ARE YOU LIVING IN SPIRITUAL POVERTY?

WHAT GOOD WILL THEY PUT ON YOUR TOMBSTONE?

WHAT'S GREEN, WITH TWO LEGS AND A TRUNK? SEASICK
TRAVELER!

WHO IS THE HEAD OF YOUR HOUSE?

WHO ARE YOUR SCAPEGOATS?

DO YOU LOVE TOO MUCH BEING YOUR OWN GOD?

DO YOU LOOK DOWN ON PEOPLE WHO LOOK DOWN ON
PEOPLE?

ARE YOU LIVING AS IF JESUS IS STILL IN THE TOMB?

WHERE WOULD YOU BE 100 YEARS FROM NOW?

HOW DOES AN INCHWORM CONVERT TO METRIC?

CAN YOU BE HIGH AND DRY?

WHAT WOULD AN IMAGINATIVE PERSON DO WITH YOUR
JOB?

IS YOUR "MISTAKES FILE" EMPTY?

IS A SODA JERK A "FIZZICIAN?"

SICK OF BEING SICK? GOD HEALS!

HOW DO YOU UNSCRAMBLE A SCRAMBLED EGG?

ARE YOU BUSY HELPING TO RIGHT SOME WRONG?

EVER HEAR OF A LUKEWARM LOCOMOTIVE?

DID YOU MAIL YOUR WIFE'S LETTER?

IF IT GOES WITHOUT SAYING, WHY SAY IT?
WHAT IS YOUR FIRST LOVE?
WHY DO MY SHARP EYES SEE CHINKS IN OTHERS' ARMOR?
ARE YOU GETTING YOUR HEAD STRAIGHT?
REMEMBER WHEN THE PENNY POSTCARD WAS 5 CENTS?
YOU LOOK LIKE A MILLION — HOW OLD *ARE* YOU?
ARE YOU MAKING THE MOST OF YOUR DAILY LIFE?
WHY DO SELF-MADE MEN MAKE SELVES THAT WAY?
IF CHILI IS HOT, WHAT IS COLD?
WHO IS BETTER BECAUSE OF YOU?
WHAT IS THE GREATEST THING YOU ARE TO DO?
WITH YOUR LIFE, IS GOD UNDERWHELMED?
STRESSED? REST IN GOD!
WHAT WILL YOU DO FOR GOD TODAY?
DO YOU SPEND GOD'S MONEY ON YOURSELF?
WHO HAS A MONOPOLY ON GOD?
ARE YOU AN "INSPIRATIONAL PERSON" TO ANYBODY?
GOD WILL FORGIVE YOU — WILL *YOU* FORGIVE YOU?
WILL ANYBODY BE IN HEAVEN BECAUSE OF YOU?
WHAT CAPTURES YOUR DETERMINATION?
WHAT ARE YOUR WORDS WORTH?
WHAT DO YOU HAVE THAT GOD NEEDS?
HAVE YOU RESISTED GOD LONG ENOUGH?
KID ON VACATION: "WHEN DO WE GO HOME AND LIVE
    HAPPILY EVER AFTER?"
REMEMBER WHEN QUESTIONS HAD ONLY TWO SIDES?
WHO DOES GOD WANT YOU TO LOVE FOR HIM TODAY?
WHAT HAVE YOU DONE TODAY THAT ONLY A CHRISTIAN
    WOULD DO?
DOES YOUR LIFE REALLY HONOR GOD?
WHO HAS DEFIED GOD AND WON?
CAN GOD COUNT ON YOU?
DOES GOD GO TO BARS?
ARE YOU TO BLAME FOR YOUR LONELINESS?
IS SOMETHING KEEPING YOU OUT OF GOD'S KINGDOM?
ARE YOU SERVING THE LORD WITH GLADNESS?
WOULD YOU PREACH WHAT YOU PRACTICE?
WHY NOT LEGALIZE CRIME AND TAX IT OUT OF BUSINESS?
    — WILL ROGERS
ARE YOU HUGGING YOURSELF TO DEATH?

IF YOUR BROTHER IS A TURKEY, WHAT ARE YOU?

IS CHRIST "LORD" OF YOUR "RELIGIOUS ACTIVITIES" ONLY?

WHAT WOULD YOU GIVE US LAST?

DO YOU THANK GOD OVER YOUR FOOD DAILY?

TEN YEARS FROM NOW WHAT WOULD YOU WISH YOU HAD DONE NOW?

DO YOU BUILD SELF UP BY TEARING OTHERS DOWN?

HOW DO YOU DO WITH ADVICE YOU GIVE OTHERS?

HOW DO YOU GET DOWN GRACEFULLY FROM A HIGH HORSE?

IS YOUR CONVERSION UP TO DATE?

SHOULD WE OBEY GOD OR POLLS?

WHERE DO YOU PAY YOUR TITHES?

WHO NEEDS LOVING? YOU DO!

WILL YOU TRUST GOD WITH YOUR REPUTATION?

ARE YOU BEING GOOD TO GOD?

WHAT SEPARATES MEN FROM BOYS? AUTO INSURANCE!

HOW ARE YOU SPENDING YOUR TALENTS?

IS YOUR LIFE JUSTIFYING YOUR BIRTH?

GOD IS LOOKING FOR MESSENGERS — YOU?

NEED ANSWERS? ASK GOD!

READY FOR A NEW BEGINNING WITH GOD?

WHO DO YOU SAY JESUS IS?

Q: "WHAT WERE YOU IN CIVILIAN LIFE?" A: "HAPPY, SIR!"

IN CRISES, ARE YOU NEITHER BLACK NOR WHITE BUT YELLOW?

CAN A CHRISTIAN EVER RETIRE?

IS GOD WITING ON YOU FOR SOMETHING?

HAVE YOU GIVEN UP THE SUPERNATURAL?

ALL WORK AND NO PLAY MAKES JACK — AND THEN?

ARE YOU WORSHIPING SOMETHING MORE THAN JESUS CHRIST?

DO YOU HAVE TIME TO LET JESUS BE YOUR FRIEND?

DO YOU LIVE AS IF YOU BELIEVE IN THE HEREAFTER?

ARE YOU WALKING IN YOUR BEST LIGHT?

WHAT IF CHRIST SHOULD COME TODAY?

WHAT IF YOUR SOUL WERE REQUIRED OF YOU?

WHAT IF YOU GAIN WHOLE WORLD AND LOSE YOUR SOUL?

WITH YOU, WHAT IS TRULY HOLY?

WHERE DID YOUR MIND COME FROM?

EVER FELT CHRISTIAN LIFE WAS ON "HOLD?"
WITH 24 HOURS TO LIVE, WHAT WOULD YOU DO?
WASN'T JESUS A LAYMAN?
SUFFERING FROM APATHY? GOD CARES!
ARE YOU GOD'S TRAVELING SALESMAN?
EVER BLEED FROM "SPUR OF THE MOMENT?"
IF MATCHES ARE MADE IN HEAVEN, WHAT ABOUT
    LIGHTERS?
ALL ONE BODY WE?
WHAT DO YOU SEND TO A SICK FLORIST?
ARE YOU SINNING MORE, ENJOYING IT LESS?
ARE YOU SEEING THE WORLD THROUGH STAINED-GLASS
    CONTACTS?
HAVE YOU EVER MADE JESUS YOUR LORD AND SAVIOR?
WHEN ARE GOODS BAD?
Q: HOW DO YOU THANK BANK FOR NEW CAR?
    A: MONTHLY!
WHO PLOWS A FIELD BY TURNING IT OVER IN HIS MIND?

CHURCH

DO YOU BELONG HERE?
THE CHURCH IS A PLACE OF LOVE.
COME IN AND LET US HELP PREPARE FOR FINALS.
CALL OUR 24-HOUR DIAL-A-PRAYER. PHONE _____.
THE MOST SEGREGATED TABLE MUST NOT BE THE LORD'S
    TABLE.
DROP IN AND HAVE YOUR FAITH LIFTED.
SEE YOU IN CHURCH SUNDAY!
WHERE DO YOU PAY YOUR TITHES?
MAKE THE WORLD OF THE BIBLE YOUR OWN.
OUR AIM IS TO BE DEEPLY CHRISTIAN.
NEED A LOVING CHURCH? HERE'S ONE!
WE ARE HERE, NOT TO BE SERVED BUT TO SERVE.
SPIRITUALLY HUNGRY? TRY OUR FARE!
OUR CHURCH IS PRAYER CONDITIONED.
A GOOD SERMON GOES OVER YOUR HEAD, HITS A NEIGH-
    BOR.
IN SALVATION CHURCH HAS CRITICS BUT NO RIVALS.
DO YOU WANT TO BE HEALED? (PRAYERS HERE, WEDNES-
    DAY NOON).
THE CHURCH EXISTS BY MISSION AS A FIRE BY BURNING!
COME AND GROW WITH US.
FOUND A CHURCH HOME YET?
SATAN JUST LOVES BUILDING PROGRAMS!
THE CHURCH CAN BETRAY JESUS BY SEEKING STATUS QUO.
WE ARE LOOKING FOR A FEW GOOD MEMBERS. YOU?
IF YOU LACK FAITH, BORROW OURS!
BIBLE WITHOUT COLLEGE IS WORTH MORE THAN COLLEGE
    WITHOUT BIBLE.
COME TO CHURCH EARLY AND GET A BACK SEAT.
WE HAVE A SIT-IN DEMONSTRATION EVERY SUNDAY
WE SEEK TO BE A CARING PEOPLE.
IS YOURS AN EXCITING CHURCH?
CHURCH — A VITAL CENTER FOR CREATIVE LIVING.
JOIN US SUNDAYS. COFFEE 9:00, SPIRITUAL FOOD ALL
    MORNING.
JANITOR: "I'VE SEEN 12 PREACHERS COME AND GO, BUT I
    STILL BELIEVE IN GOD!"

70

TRY US — YOU'LL LIKE US!
CHRISTIAN WITH OUT CHURCH IS LIKE BEE WITHOUT HIVE.
SEEN ON QUESTIONNAIRE — CHURCH PREFERENCE:
GOTHIC.
CHURCHES MUSTN'T EXIST FOR THEIR OWN MEMBERSHIP.
OUR CHURCH HAS STANDBYERS AND BYSTANDERS.
WE'RE NOT FANCY, BUT SHORE ARE FRIENDLY!
EVERY CHURCH SHOULD HAVE A SCOUT TROOP TO BLAME
IT ON.
A SELF-CENTERED CHURCH IS UN-CHRISTIAN TOO!
WHAT ARE YOU TEACHING BY SENDING KIDS TO SUNDAY
SCHOOL?
KID AT SUNDAY SCHOOL: "WE LEARNED TO LOVE GOD AND
SIT DOWN, SIT DOWN, SIT DOWN."
A TRUE CHURCH: CHRIST'S CHURCH.
WE COULD BE YOUR CHURCH HOME!
DO YOU BRING ONLY YOUR CLOTHES TO CHURCH?
A POOR LISTENER HEARS A FEW GOOD SERMONS.
"CREATE IN ME A CLEAN HEART, O GOD!"
WHAT'S EXCITING IN YOUR CHURCH?
THE BIBLE SAYS YOU ARE SUPREMELY DEAR TO GOD.
WE SEEK TO COMFORT THE AFFLICTED, AFFLICT THE
COMFORTABLE.
PITY PARTIES HELD HERE ON DEMAND.
EVEN THE CHURCH IS NO SUBSTITUTE FOR GOD!
WE EMPHASIZE THE WARM HEART AND THE TRAINED MIND.
THE PERFECT CHURCH WOULDN'T HAVE YOU. JOIN OURS!
THE CHURCH IS TO SET THE WORLD ON FIRE!
FORMAL WORSHIP CORRECTS FEW FAULTY LIVES.
COME TO OUR REAL HAPPY HOUR. SUNDAYS 9:00 A.M.
THIS IS THE CHURCH OF INSTANT "AT-HOMENESS."
SOME GO TO CHURCH TO SEE WHO DIDN'T.
IN THIS CHURCH WE EXCEED ALL OTHERS IN HUMILITY.
THE NEW YEAR OFFERS 52 APPOINTMENTS WITH GOD.
WE ARE EXCITED ABOUT BEING DISCIPLES!
WE'RE DISCOVERING THE NEW CONTINENT OF THE SPIRIT!
CHURCH IS "LIFE TOGETHER" UNDER THE AUTHORITY OF
GOD. — BONHOEFFER.

CHRISTIAN

BEING CHRISTIAN SIMPLE, YES; EASY, NO!
NOBODY IS BORN A CHRISTIAN.
REALLY TO LIVE, DENY SELF, TAKE UP CROSS, FOLLOW JESUS.
A CHRISTIAN IS ONE WHO FEELS RESPONSIBLE.
"SAVED" IS LIVING IN THE BELIEF THAT WE ARE LOVED.
REPENT!
LIVE AND HELP LIVE.
CHRISTIANS: LOOK IN THE BACK OF BIBLE — WE WIN!
IN HEAVEN — NO BAPTISTS, PRESBYTERIANS, METHODISTS
    — ONLY CHRISTIANS.
CONFESSION IS THE FIRST STEP TO REPENTANCE.
CHRISTIANS NEED THE FLOCK!
CONVERSION IS AN INSIDE JOB!
A CHRISTIAN IS A SOLDIER UNDER ORDERS.
CHRISTIANS HAVE NO ROOM FOR EXPEDIENCE!
PROBLEMS OF THE SOUL ARE SETTLED IN THE SOUL.
WE CAN'T ACCEPT GOD'S LOVE UNTIL WE REPENT!
CHARACTER IS EASIER KEPT THAN RECOVERED.
FOR CHRISTIANS, LOVE IS NOT AN OPTION.
"HERE AM I, LORD — SEND ME!
BLESSED ARE THE HUMBLE.
YOUR JOB IS TO SPREAD THE WORD.
CHRISTIAN: ONE WHO KNOWS HE'S BEEN FORGIVEN.
TREASURED BELIEFS NEED STEADY ATTENTION.
IF YOU CAN'T BE CHRISTIAN HERE, YOU CAN'T ANYWHERE.
HATE THE EVIL, LOVE THE GOOD.
"I KNOW THAT MY REDEEMER LIVES!"
CHRISTIANS PROTECT INNOCENT PEOPLE FROM HURT.
CHRISTIANS ARE COMMITTED TO CHRIST IN INTEGRITY.
DIVINE LAW: WHAT YOU SOW, YOU REAP!
FROM THOSE WHO HAVE MUCH, MUCH IS REQUIRED.
CHRISTIANITY GROWS ONLY WHEN PUT INTO PRACTICE.
CHRISTIAN: GROW OLD WITH ME, THE BEST IS YET TO BE.
A HALF-BELIEVER IS NO BELIEVER.
DON'T SOOTHE CONSCIENCE WITH SOFT LIES!
IT IS ONE THING TO PRAISE DISCIPLINE; ANOTHER, TO SUB-
    MIT.
THERE IS A WAY AND A NOT-THE-WAY.

THE BIG QUESTION FOR CHRISTIANS — INTEGRITY.

A REAL CHRISTIAN HAS A STRONG FAMILY LIKENESS TO JESUS CHRIST.

NO ONE IS BORN A CHRISTIAN — WE CHOOSE.

CHRISTIANS HAVE ONLY TWO RIGHTS — LOVE AND FORGIVE.

THE DYING NEVER SAY THEY ARE SORRY THEY WERE CHRISTIAN!

BE NOT SIMPLY GOOD, BUT GOOD FOR SOMETHING!

CONSCIENCE IS THE LORD'S SEARCHLIGHT.

DISCIPLINE IS COSTLY BUT WORTH IT.

"HE WHO WINS SOULS IS WISE." PROVERBS 11:30

A USED-CAR SALESMAN CAN BE A CHRISTIAN.

ALL IS SPOILED WITH UNSURRENDERED SELF AT CENTER.

YOUR CHARACTER IS REVEALED BY WHAT YOU SAY.

OUR SOULS ARE RESTLESS UNTIL THEY REST IN HIM. (AUGUSTINE)

CHRISTIANS ARE ADVENTURERS AND EXPLORERS.

COSTLY GRACE IS TO GIVE LIFE FOR OTHERS.

AFTER CONVERSION: "I FEEL SO LIGHT!"

IN TERMS OF ETERNITY, WHAT ARE YOUR WORDS WORTH?

CONVERSION: LIKE A RIVER, NOT A POINT.

CONVERSION: RESPONSE TO FLOW OF GOD'S COMPASSION.

HEAVEN REJOICES WHEN WRONG BECOMES RIGHT.

IT'S EASIER TO PREACH THAN TO PRACTICE.

BE AN INSTRUMENT OF GOD'S PEACE.

BE BEAUTIFUL OF SOUL AND LET OTHERS SEE IN.

THE TESTING OF FAITH LEADS TO ENDURANCE.

TODAY, HELP GOD BIND THE WOUNDS ON PEOPLE'S SOULS.

CHRISTIANITY IS THE LIFE THAT LASTS!

TRY OVERCOMING EVIL WITH GOOD.

STAY IN THE LIGHT!

FOR A CHRISTIAN NOTHING IS WASTED IN LIFE.

YOUR WIFE CAN'T TAKE CARE OF YOUR RELIGION!

HE WHO GETS MUCH WILL ACCOUNT FOR MUCH.

BEING BORN IN A CHRISTIAN HOME DOESN'T MAKE YOU A CHRISTIAN.

OUR AIM IS TO BE DEEPLY CHRISTIAN.

CHRISTIANS ARE BLOOD BROTHERS! AND SISTERS!

SOME CHANGE WAYS WHEN THEY SEE LIGHT, OTHERS WHEN THEY FEEL HEAT.

RESISTANCE TO DISEASE DEPENDS ON THE QUALITY OF LIVING.

BETTER BE A SERMON THAN PREACH ONE.

THERE IS A RIGHT WAY AND A WRONG WAY.

A SAINT MAKES GOODNESS ATTRACTIVE.

A PERSON WOULD DO NOTHING IF HE WAITED UNTIL HE COULD DO IT SO WELL THAT NO ONE COULD FIND FAULT.

TODAY'S CROSS IS WHERE HUMAN NEED IS.

EARLY CHRISTIANS: THOSE UP AT 5 A.M.

CONSCIENCE IS WHAT HURTS WHEN ALL ELSE FEELS GOOD

SATAN WANTS US TO SEE MORALITY AS RELATIVE.

HEAVEN NEVER FORGETS ITS FAITHFUL.

CONCEIT IS A GREAT SPIRITUAL ENEMY.

THE CROSS BELONGS IN THE CENTER OF THE MARKETPLACE.

CHARACTER IS WHAT YOU ARE ON VACATION.

IT'S HARD FOR THE RICH TO ENTER THE KINGDOM.

MOST DANGEROUS DECEPTION — SELF DECEPTION.

YOU CAN'T HAVE 'GOD-IN-YOU' WITH 'YOU-IN-YOU.'

THE KINGDOM IS WITHIN — AFRAID TO LOOK?

"BE CLOTHED WITH HUMILITY."

WE WALK THE WAY WE TALK.

THOU SHALT NOT CUSS!

LONELINESS SHARED IS LONELINESS LOST.

THE LAST JUDGMENT TAKES PLACE EVERY DAY.

THE SOUL OF AMERICA IS TORN BETWEEN CHRISTIAN AND PAGAN.

THE EYES ARE THE WINDOWS OF THE SOUL.

NATURE IS SACRAMENTAL TO THE SAINT.

IN THE KINGDOM, THE GREATEST IS LIKE A CHILD.

THE TEN COMMANDMENTS SAY WE REAP WHAT WE SOW.

PEOPLE DO NOT IMPROVE WITH SELF AS ONLY MODEL.

THE BLESSED LEAVE LOVE WHEREVER THEY GO.

REPENT MEANS, "HAVE ANOTHER MIND."

TO ENTER HEAVEN, LET HEAVEN ENTER YOU.

THIS IS THE PLACE FOR HEALING OF HUMAN HEARTS.

ELEVENTH HOUR CONVERSION IS USELESS IF YOU DIE AT 10:30.

TO AVOID LIVING BY THE GOSPEL SPEND MUCH TIME ON DOCTRINE.

IT IS EASIER TO SEE CLOSED THAN OPEN DOORS.

THE GOSPEL IS DEEP SPEAKING TO DEEP!

THE SPIRITUAL PERSON WORKS AT LISTENING.

ONLY GOD CAN SATISFY A HUNGRY HUMAN HEART.

STORMS TEST STRENGTH OF YOUR ANCHOR.

START WITH LITTLE HILLS FIRST.

WE JUDGE OURSELVES BY INTENTION, OTHERS BY PERFORMANCE!

THE PURE IN HEART SEE THROUGH SPIRITUAL EYES.

SATAN DOESN'T SAY, "FOLLOW ME" — BUT RATHER "EXPRESS YOURSELF."

THE OLD RUGGED CROSS MAY BE POPULAR BECAUSE IT IS ON A HILL AND FAR AWAY!

MAN SYMBOLIZES AND QUICKLY WORSHIPS THE SYMBOL.

A TRUE SPIRITUAL EXPERIENCE CORRECTS FAULTS OF CHARACTER.

FROM THE ABUNDANCE OF THE HEART, THE MOUTH SPEAKS.

TEMPTATION SAYS, "BE YOURSELF."

A CHRISTIAN IS A LIFE TERMER!

AS ONE THINKS IN HIS HEART, SO IS HE!

ALL THINGS ARE POSSIBLE TO THOSE WHO BELIEVE!

FREEDOM OF WORSHIP IS NOT NEGLECT OF WORSHIP.

THE HEART HAS EYES THE HEAD KNOWS NOT OF.

VALID QUESTION: "FRIEND, ARE YOU SAVED?"

INTEGRITY COMES FROM YEARS OF PATIENT WELL-DOING.

REVIVAL WISDOM: "IT AIN'T HOW HIGH THEY JUMPS, BUT WHAT THEY DOES WHEN THEY GITS DOWN"!

HEAR YOUR ENEMIES — THEY ARE THE FIRST TO FIND FAULT.

CONSCIENCE HAS A THOUSAND TONGUES.

LIFE UNDER THE CROSS MEANS RELENTLESS REFORMATION.

LOOK NOT FOR PRETTY FACE BUT FOR CHARACTER AND GRACE.

WHEN YOU GIVE UP, GOD CAN BEGIN!

"BEING SAVED" IS A PROCESS, NOT AN ARRIVAL.

IT'S HARD TO SERVE GOD AND STATUS.

DON'T LIVE ON GARBAGE WHEN YOU COULD HAVE SOUL FOOD.

USE TO THE LIMITS THE POWERS GOD GRANTS YOU.

"HE WHO ENDURES TO THE END WILL BE SAVED."

REGRET CAN BE AN AWFUL WASTE OF TIME.

SELF-CENTERED IS OFF-CENTERED.

ONLY THE GRACE OF GOD CAN REALLY RENEW LIFE.

THE EARLY CHRISTIAN CHURCH WAS PRO-LIFE.

DON'T BE OVERCOME WITH EVIL. OVERCOME IT WITH GOOD.

A CANDLE LOSES NOTHING BY LIGHTING ANOTHER.

CHRISTIANITY IS LETTING LOVE REPRODUCE ITSELF IN US.

CHARACTER IS WHAT YOU ARE IF NEVER FOUND OUT.

IT'S HOW WELL YOU LIVE THAT MATTERS.

RELIGION IS LIKE SOAP: THOSE NEED MOST, USE LEAST.

FOR EVIL TO WIN, LET THE GOOD DO NOTHING!

"PUT ON THE WHOLE ARMOUR OF GOD — DAILY."

PRESENT SUFFERINGS ARE NOT EQUAL TO THE GLORY TO BE.

CHRISTIANITY: LETTING LOVE BE REPRODUCED IN US.

GOOD RELIGION IS CONTAGIOUS.

BE BEAUTIFUL OF SOUL AND LET OTHERS SEE INTO YOUR SOUL.

THE STRONG MUST HELP THE WEAK.

LET US BE AT LEAST AS EVANGELICAL AS THE PAGANS ARE!

HEAVEN IS NOT REACHED IN A SINGLE BOUND.

WHERE I GO, MY CHARACTER GOES TOO.

CHRISTIANS ARE BRANDED BY GOD.

SOMETIMES SWALLOW PRIDE AND EAT CROW.

WALK THE WALK AS WELL AS TALK THE TALK.

TO CHRISTIANS ALL GROUND IS HOLY GROUND!

CHRISTIANS BUY SCIENCE, BUT GO BEYOND!

LIVE UP TO YOUR VOWS IF IT KILLS YOU!

SUCCESS, FAILURE, STRUGGLE

SUCCESS IS FAILURE TURNED INSIDE OUT.
LORD, HELP ME TO HANG IN THERE.
SUCCESS REQUIRES GIVING YOUR WHOLE SELF.
SUCCESS MAY BE ONLY AN INSPIRATION AWAY.
DO YOU KNOW A VICTORY WHEN YOU SEE ONE?
SUCCESS IS NOT ALWAYS A STEADY CLIMB UPWARD.
SUCCESS AND FAILURE ARE HERO AND SIDEKICK.
NO MAN IS A SUCCESS WHO ISN'T ENJOYING LIFE.
WE DO LITTLE WORTH DOING BY ACCIDENT.
TO ACHIEVE, PEOPLE OFTEN HAVE TO BE STIRRED UP.
TODAY: ACCENTUATE THE POSITIVE.
GETTING ON IS GETTING UP EACH TIME YOU'RE DOWN.
ATTITUDE MORE THAN APTITUDE DETERMINES SUCCESS.
TRY WANTING WHAT YOU HAVE.
COMMIT TO GOD WHAT HE CAN JOYFULLY BLESS AND
    YOUR PLANS WILL SUCCEED.
THE CROSS IS FAILURE MADE SUCCESS.
THE RULES OF SUCCESS WORK ONLY IF YOU DO.
SMART PEOPLE DON'T SOLVE PROBLEMS PART WAY.
THE NEGLECTED OPPORTUNITY WON'T COME BACK.
CALL GOD'S RESCUE SQUAD TO FREE YOU FROM TEMPTA-
    TIONS.
YOU'RE NOT A FAILURE UNTIL YOU BLAME SOMEONE ELSE.
GOALS GIVE YOU A TRACK TO RUN ON.
STRESSED STRESS STRESSES MORE!
IF YOU FAIL, FAIL GALLANTLY!
A THOROUGHLY SATISFIED MAN IS PROBABLY A FAILURE.
DEFEAT SOMETIMES SHAKES SOULS TO LET GLORY OUT.
UNSOLVED PROBLEMS ARE GOD'S LANGUAGE.
 PLACE IN THE SUN SOMETIMES BRINGS BLISTERS.
GOLD IS TRIED BY FIRE; BRAVERY BY ADVERSITY.
SUCCESS IS LEAVING THE WORLD BETTER THAN YOU
    FOUND IT.
A FAILURE BLAMES OTHERS FOR HIS MISTAKES.
FAILURE: PATH OF LEAST RESISTANCE.
EACH DAY YOU SET AN EXAMPLE FOR YOUR GREAT, GREAT
    GRANDCHILDREN.

IN SELF-RIGHTEOUSNESS WE ALWAYS WIN.
SUFFERING CAN PURIFY.
SUFFERING CAN FORCE US TO AN HONEST EVALUATION.
SUFFERING FOSTERS MERCY, SYMPATHY, UNDERSTANDING.
SUFFERING CAN PERFECT AND ENNOBLE CHARACTER.
NEVER FORGET: GOD IS GOOD!
CLOUDS PRODUCE RAINBOWS.
GOD DOESN'T LEAVE US TO SUFFER ALONE.
IT IS BEST TO CLEAN OUT ONE'S OWN THISTLES FIRST.
CHRIST SUFFERS OUR PAIN.
LOOK BEYOND SCIENCE FOR COMFORT.
WHEN IN PAIN, LOOK FOR GOD'S PLAN.
PAIN ANNOUNCES "YOU ARE MORTAL."
SIGNS OF HEART DISEASE: EVIL THOUGHTS.
SATAN SEDUCES. OUR JOB TO RESIST.
HISTORY IS UNDER GOD'S SOVEREIGNTY.
JESUS IS REMEMBERED BECAUSE HE ROSE FROM DEATH.

SEASONS

LIVING THANKS IS EVEN BETTER THAN GIVING THANKS.
GLORY BE TO GOD ON HIGH, AND TO THE EARTH BE PEACE.
IF HE DOESN'T LIKE THE GIFT TIE, GIVE HIM A SOCK!
MISTLETOE IS BAD FOR TREES, FUN FOR TWOS.
THE STAR OF BETHLEHEM WILL NEVER SET.
THE DEAREST CHRISTMAS IS CHRISTMAS IN THE HEART.
CHRISTMAS CHEER COMES FROM DISPENSING CHEER.
GIVE BIBLES FOR CHRISTMAS.
IF YOU CAN'T BE A STAR IN THE SKY, BE A CANDLE.
THE WORLD'S BEST NEWS IS FROM A GRAVEYARD.
CHRISTMAS IN THE HEART PUTS CHRISTMAS IN THE AIR.
THE BEST GIFTS ARE TIED WITH HEARTSTRINGS.
NEW YEAR'S EVE WE BLOW HORN INSTEAD OF TOP.
THE NIGHT BEFORE CHRISTMAS . . . NOT A CREATURE WAS
    STIRRING . . . NEEDED BATTERIES.
THE CHRISTMAS GIFT RACE ENDED IN A TIE.
BE THANKFUL YOU'RE NOT A TURKEY.
GOOD FRIDAY IS GOD'S GOODNESS OVERCOMING MAN'S
    BADNESS.
CHRISTMAS IS JESUS' BIRTHDAY — PROBABLY NOT YOURS!
DON'T FREEZE FREEDOM — PRESERVE IT!
CHRISTMAS IS TIDINGS OF COMFORT AND JOY.
A THANKFUL SPIRIT IS LIKE SUNSHINE ON THE FIELDS.
ON THANKSGIVING WE ACKNOWLEDGE OUR DEPEN-
    DENCE.
GOD'S FATHERHOOD COST HIM THE CROSS.
AN OLD CHRISTMAS CUSTOM IS GETTING IN DEBT.
ALWAYS AT CHRISTMAS THERE'S A SONG IN THE AIR.
LITTLE GIRL: MY DADDY IS ONE OF THE THREE WISE GUYS
    FROM THE EAST.
CHRISTMAS IS MORE THAN A VISIT TO DISNEYLAND.
IS CHRIST IN YOUR CHRISTMAS PLANS?
REPENT AND GOD WILL HEAL THE LAND!
REMEMBER: GOD BECAME A BABY!
IS THERE ROOM FOR HIM IN YOUR INN?
AT CHRISTMAS THE SHEPHERDS GLORIFIED GOD — DO
    YOU?

WISE MEN STILL FOLLOW THE STAR.

WISE MEN STILL ADORE HIM.

EASTER IS NOT DECORATION DAY.

LIVE AS IF EVERY DAY WAS CHRISTMAS.

EASTER! COME! SEE! GO! TELL!

IF YOU CAN'T BE A STAR IN THE SKY BE A LAMP IN THE NIGHT.

"THE HIGH PRIEST" SHOWED HOW LOW HUMANITY CAN GO.

EASTER BEGINS A NEW ORDER.

A SHEPHERD IN MATTRESS FACTORY WATCHES FLOCK BY NIGHT.

WHO WILL CLEAN UP AFTER THE REINDEER?

SOME HALLOWEEN PUMPKINS ARE NOW CALLED JILL-O-LANTERNS.

LITTLE BOY: I'M GIVING UP SOAP FOR LENT."

GOD GAVE US MEMORIES THAT WE MIGHT HAVE ROSES IN DECEMBER.

GOD'S WILL WILL NEVER LEAD YOU WHERE GOD'S GRACE CANNOT KEEP YOU!

WHAT ARE YOU GIVING UP FOR LENT?

CONSTANT RENEWAL COMES FROM CONSTANT THANKS-GIVING.

"WHAT SHALL I GIVE HIM"? GIVE HIM YOUR HEART.

SANTA: "DOC, I DON'T BELIEVE IN MYSELF!"

POOR WAY TO CELEBRATE 4TH — BUYING A FIFTH.

EASTER IS A TIME OF BLESSED CERTAINTY.

SOME RESOLUTIONS GO IN ONE YEAR AND OUT THE OTHER.

STAGES OF SANTA: BELIEVES IN, DOESN'T, IS.

BETWEEN EASTER AND CHRISTMAS GOD IS NOT DEAD OR ASLEEP.

ONE SWALLOW DOESN'T MAKE SUMMER BUT BREAKS NEW YEAR'S RESOLUTION.

EASTER IS LIFE; HERE AND HEREAFTER!

CHURCH SIGN: STOP HERE FOR HOLIDAY SPIRITS.

JOY, HAPPINESS

DON'T MISS HAPPINESS BY NOT STOPPING TO ENJOY IT!
SOME CAUSE HAPPINESS WHERE THEY GO — OTHERS,
    WHEN.
THE ROAD TO HAPPINESS IS UNDER CONSTRUCTION.
THERE CAN BE JOY EVEN IN TRIBULATION!
JOY IS AN INSIDE JOB!
HAPPY IS HE WHO SUFFERS FOR WHAT IS RIGHT!
HE IS HAPPIEST WHO IS HAPPY AT HOME.
WHAT GOOD IS HAPPINESS? CAN'T BUY MONEY WITH IT!
PRACTICE HAPPINESS LIKE A VIOLIN.
HAPPINESS DOESN'T COME BY SEEKING IT.
ARE YOU HAPPY WITH WHAT YOU'RE DOING FOR GOD?
HAPPINESS AND BEAUTY ARE BOTH BY-PRODUCTS.
HAPPINESS IS A VEGETARIAN STUDYING MEAT PRICES.
"THE JOY OF THE LORD IS YOUR STRENGTH."
"HAPPY ARE THOSE WHO HEAR THE WORD AND OBEY IT!"
JOY IS THE ECHO OF GOD'S LIFE IN US.
THE SEARCH FOR HAPPINESS IS A SOURCE OF UNHAPPINESS.
PURSUIT OF HAPPINESS -- WHAT IF YOU GET IT?
HAPPINESS IS A BY-PRODUCT OF SEEKING GOD.
HAPPIEST ARE THOSE TOO BUSY TO NOTE WHETHER OR
    NOT!
HAPPINESS IS LIKE CHASING A BUTTERFLY.
HAPPINESS IS NOT A STATION — IT'S A WAY OF TRAVELING.
TO BE HAPPY, MAKE OTHERS HAPPY!
"A MERRY HEART IS GOOD MEDICINE" — PROVERBS.
TO BE HAPPY EVER AFTER, DON'T BE AFTER TOO MUCH!
REAL JOY COMES FROM DOING THE WORTHWHILE.

CHRISTIAN SERVICE

CHRISTIAN LIFE IS LIKE PLANE RIDE: STOP AND YOU DROP.
WE'LL HELP YOU PREPARE FOR YOUR FINALS.
PEOPLE WILL MOSTLY BELIEVE WHAT YOU DO.
HELP SOMEBODY TODAY AND TRUST GOD WITH TOMOR-
ROW.
TO GET RID OF LONELINESS, SERVE THE LONELY.
YOU CAN'T BE A BEACON IF YOUR LIGHT WON'T SHINE.
BEAUTIFUL SENTIMENTS WEIGH LESS THAN LOVELY
ACTION.
GOD CARES AND WE CARE.
PRESENT YOUR BODY A LIVING SACRIFICE.
CHRISTIANS GET A NEW DIRECTION, NEW SPIRIT, NEW
SPHERE OF LIVING.
AS WE HELP ONE ANOTHER WITH TEMPTATIONS, GOD
HELPS US.
LIFE ON THIS PLANET IS BASED ON CONVERSIONS.
GO TO YOUR CHURCH AND FIND STRENGTH FOR YOUR LIFE.
THE KINGDOM BEGINS WHEN WE LOSE OURSELVES.
CHRISTIANS ARE TO TRUST AND OBEY.
WE ARE HERE NOT TO BE SERVED, BUT TO SERVE.
DISCUSSING MY HUNGER DOESN'T FEED ME!
TO STOP BEING BORED, DO SOMETHING GOOD FOR SOME-
BODY.
TODAY — SOMEBODY LONELY NEEDS YOU.
YOU CAN'T HAVE YOUR SOUL AND SAVE IT TOO.
YOU ARE YOUR BROTHER'S BROTHER!
"CHRISTIAN" IS NOT WHIPPING UP THE WILL BUT SUR-
RENDERING IT.
SPEND SOME TIME ALONE FOR PEACE.
FEW LIVE AS THEY BELIEVE.
"FEED THE HUNGRY, CLOTHE THE NAKED."
LONELINESS IS A PRISON: SHARE YOUR FELLOWSHIP.
ILLUSION: THAT YOU CAN SERVE SELF AND BE DEEPLY
HAPPY.
ARE YOU LIVING IN HALF-CONVERSION, WALKING IN HALF-
LIGHT?
HELP SOMEBODY TODAY.

SERVICE GROWS OUT OF WHAT YOU ARE.

WEIGH NEIGHBOR IN SAME BALANCE YOU WEIGH SELF.

DENY YOURSELF: PUT DOWN YOUR SPOON; FEED THE
HUNGRY.

"THERE'S GOING TO BE A QUIZ AT YOUR ASCENSION" —
GODSPELL)

LAY NOT UP TREASURES ON EARTH, BUT IN HEAVEN.

THE RICH MUST LIVE MORE SIMPLY THAT THE POOR MAY
SIMPLY LIVE.

WE HAVE A MORAL RESPONSIBILITY TO RESIST INJUSTICE.

"WHEN YOU GONNA WAKE UP AND STRENGTHEN THINGS
THAT REMAIN?" — DYLAN.

A HUMANIST STATE DOES NOT TOLERATE ANY GOD BUT
ITSELF.

IN SOME COUNTRIES, PARENTS ARE NOT ALLOWED TO
TEACH ABOUT JESUS, WOULD YOU BE AT HOME THERE?

TRUTH/TRUTHS

JESUS SPEAKS TRUTH TO YOU. LISTEN.
GOD'S TRUTH WILL MAKE YOU FREE.
JESUS IS THE TRUTH.
TO ADD TO THE TRUTH IS TO SUBTRACT FROM IT.
WHEN SPEAKING TRUTH, SPEAK IT IN LOVE.
WHITE LIES LEAD TO COLOR BLINDNESS.
YOU HAVE TO KNOW THE TRUTH BEFORE IT CAN MAKE YOU
    FREE.
A LIE A DAY DRIVES GOD'S SPIRIT AWAY.
TRUTH IS NOT AT ALL AFRAID TO RELATE TO LIFE.
IT TAKES OPEN EYES TO SEE THE TRUTH.
JUSTICE IS TRUTH IN ACTION.
DISCIPLES KNOW THE TRUTH WHICH MAKES US FREE.
IT IS POSSIBLE TO LIE WITH THE TRUTH! SATAN DID!
HALF TRUTHS WILL NOT MAKE YOU FREE.
DIGGING FOR THE FACTS IS BETTER THAN JUMPING TO
    CONCLUSIONS.
WE SHINE LESS AFTER GLOSSING THE TRUTH.
THOUGHT: THE GREATEST THIEF IS ONE WHO WILL ROB
    YOU OF THE TRUTH — WATSON.
REMEMBER THAT WE DO SEE IN PART AND THROUGH A
    GLASS DARKLY.
SCARCE AS TRUTH IS, SUPPLY STILL EXCEEDS DEMAND.
EXAGGERATION: TRUTH THAT HAS LOST ITS TEMPER.
SIN HAS AN I IN THE MIDDLE.
WHAT WE BECOME IS OUR GIFT TO GOD.
WHAT YOU CAN'T CURE YOU MUST ENDURE.
THE CROSS OVERCAME EVIL WITH GOOD.
NOT TO DECIDE IS TO DECIDE.
AT LEAST THE CONCEITED DON'T TALK ABOUT OTHERS.
IT IS EASIEST TO BE BRAVE FROM A SAFE DISTANCE.
TIME TO RELAX: WHEN YOU DON'T HAVE IT.
IT COSTS A LOT TO DIE COMFORTABLY.
NOTHING CAN SEPARATE US FROM THE LOVE OF GOD BUT
    OURSELVES.
POSITIVE: WRONG AT THE TOP OF YOUR LUNGS. —
    (AMBROSE BIERCE)

84

HOME/FAMILY

OF ALL HOME REMEDIES A GOOD MOTHER IS BEST.
THINK OF MARRIAGE AS A SORT OF BASE CAMP.
IT TAKES TWO TO CARRY THE HEAVY CHAIN OF WEDLOCK.
"GOOD" FAMILIES ARE OFTEN WORSE THAN THE OTHERS.
MARRIED MEN MAKE THE BEST HUSBANDS.
MANY A FAMILY TREE COULD STAND TRIMMING.
BEST GIFT: FAMILY WRAPPED UP IN EACH OTHER.
DECIDE DAILY TO SAY "I DO" TO LOVE.
CALL "TIME OUT"; HUDDLE WITH FAMILY.
DON'T WAIT; TELL YOUR CHILD "I LOVE YOU."
GIVE YOURSELF SEVEN POINTS IF TOLD SOMEBODY "I LOVE
    YOU" TODAY.
CREDIT YOURSELF SEVEN POINTS FOR THAT SOFT ANSWER.
WHO IS SPIRITUAL HEAD OF YOUR FAMILY?
IS YOUR MATE PERFECT? ARE YOU?
GOOD HOME REMEDY: EQUAL PARTS LOVE AND FORGIVE-
    NESS.
GOD FORGIVES; WILL YOU?
A PERFECT MARRIAGE REQUIRES TWO IMPERFECT PEOPLE.
DON'T JUST TOLERATE: LOVE YOUR MATE.
SUBTRACT SEVEN POINTS IF YOU YELLED AT SOMEONE
    TODAY.
FAMILY POLES APART? CHANGE YOUR NEGATIVES TO GOD'S
    POSITIVES.
BEST FAMILY READING: THE BIBLE.
TOO BUSY TO READ BIBLE? GET TAPES!
A FISHWIFE COULD BE A CATFISH.
THINK POSITIVES ABOUT YOUR FAMILY.
DIVORCE CAUSED BY HARD HEARTS: KEEP YOURS PLIABLE
    . . . WITH PRAYER.
CHILDREN NEED PARENTS . . . IN CHURCH!
DON'T SERVE ROAST PREACHER TO CHILDREN. THAT
    STUNTS GROWTH.
IS HOME A FIGHTING RING? GOD WILL REFEREE.
A MARRIAGE NEEDS REBUILDING EVERY DAY.
MARRIAGE IS MADE IN HEAVEN, BUT PEOPLE ARE RESPON-
    SIBLE FOR MAINTENANCE.

DON'T CRITICIZE WIFE'S JUDGMENT — LOOK WHO SHE
    MARRIED!
NOTE: UGLY FAMILIES KEEP NEGATIVES IN FAMILY ALBUMS.
USUALLY QUARRELS ARE WITH WELL-FROZEN WORDS.
MISGUIDED SEX LEADS DOWN DARK ALLEYS.
KID: "MOM, WHERE DO ELEPHANTS COME FROM?"
IF WOMAN'S INTUITION IS SO GOOD, WHY ARE THERE SO
    MANY QUESTIONS?
SUCCESS IN MARRIAGE IS BEING THE RIGHT PERSON.
THE PROPER TIME TO INFLUENCE THE CHARACTER OF A
    CHILD IS ABOUT 100 YEARS BEFORE HE IS BORN —
    WILLIAM RALPH INGE.
BE A MODEL HUSBAND — A WORKING MODEL.
WHEN THE RIGHT GIRL COMES ALONG, SHE'LL TELL YOU.
BIGAMISTS HAVE TWO MOTHERS-IN-LAW.
IT ONLY TAKES ONE TO START A QUARREL.
LIKE DIETS, MARRIAGES ARE RUINED WITH A DISH ON THE
    SIDE.
A HAPPY FAMILY IS AN EARLIER HEAVEN.
MOTHER TO CHILD WHO HAS MISBEHAVED: "WHAT AM I
    GOING TO DO WITH YOU?"
    CHILD: "FORGIVE ME?"
TO CALL WIFE "RELATIVE BY MARRIAGE" IS NO EXCUSE.
TO FIND OUT WHAT SHE THINKS OF YOU, MARRY HER!
BIRDS FLY SOUTH IN WINTER — A FAMILY TRADITION.
IS THERE A CEREAL TO SAP KIDS' ENERGY?
WHY NOT BIGAMY? NO MAN CAN SERVE TWO MASTERS!
POOR GIRL, ALWAYS BRIDE, NEVER BRIDESMAID.
SWEETEST THING IN LIFE: WELCOME OF A WIFE.
THE FIRST IN THE BATHTUB IS CALLED RINGLEADER.
KID: "DAD, DOES M-I-R-A-G-E SPELL MARRIAGE?"
FOR DIVIDENDS, INVEST TIME IN YOUR MARRIAGE.
"AS FOR HOUSEWORK, I LIKE NOTHING BETTER."
MARRIAGE IS A SACRAMENT.
"BOY, DID I GIVE HER A GOOD LISTENING TO!"
TRY PRAISING WIFE EVEN IF IT FRIGHTENS HER AT FIRST.
THE MAN WHO NEVER MADE A MISTAKE MARRIED A WIFE
    WHO DID!
DOES YOUR MATE DESERVE A BETTER MATE?
FAMILY GLUE: PRAY WITHOUT CEASING!

MARRIAGE MAKES TWO ONE — THEN COMES THE WORLD SERIES TO SEE WHO'S "ONE."

MARRIAGES ARE USUALLY HAPPY — IT'S LIVING TOGETHER THAT CAUSES TROUBLE.

AT HOME ALL ARE LAYMEN!

"HUSBANDS, LOVE YOU WIFE AS CHRIST LOVES THE CHURCH."

BABIES ARE SUBJECT TO CHANGE WITHOUT NOTICE.

FOR MOTHERS THE SON ALWAYS SHINES.

IT TAKES EFFORT TO BE AGREEABLE.

A CHILD'S FIRST SCHOOL IS THE FAMILY.

"HE'S THE KIND WHO LOVES HIS WIFE'S HUSBAND BEST."

NOTHING IS OPENED BY MISTAKE MORE THAN THE MOUTH!

DOES YOUR WIFE BEAR ALL THE BURDEN FOR YOUR FAMILY?

IN BACKWARD COUNTRIES KIDS STILL OBEY THEIR PARENTS.

MAN IN LOVE WITH DIMPLE MISTAKEN TO MARRY WHOLE GIRL.

MASTER OF HOUSE, I HAVE READ: FIRST ONE UP, LAST TO BED.

A SMALL HOUSE IS BETTER THAN A BIG MORTGAGE.

IS EVERYTHING AT HOME CONTROLLED BY SWITCHES EXCEPT KIDS?

THE FAMILY THAT SMOKES TOGETHER CHOKES TOGETHER!

KIDS INHERIT THE VIRTUES OF MOTHER AS WELL AS THE SINS OF DAD.

MARRIAGE HAS PAINS BUT CELIBACY FEW PLEASURES.

MOST KIDS ARE BASICALLY SOUND.

IT'S STILL VALID TO HONOR FATHER AND MOTHER.

THE QUARREL WAS OVER WHEN WE AGREED I WAS WRONG!

LOOKING AT DIVORCE RATE: MANY SAYING "I DO" DON'T!

BABIES COST A LOT BUT THINK HOW LONG THEY LAST!

HOW'S IT IN THE SOUL OF YOUR MARRIAGE?

DISCIPLINING CHILDREN IS TO SHOW THEM LOVE.

TABLE GRACE MAKES MEALS A SACRAMENT.

THE BIRTH OF A CHILD SAYS "GOD'S NOT THROUGH."

NEGLECT IS A COMMON FORM OF CHILD ABUSE.

IF YOU REALLY LOVED ME YOU'D HAVE MARRIED SOMEONE ELSE!

ONE GOOD TURN GETS MOST OF BLANKET.

PRAYER CAN RAISE YOUR BOILING POINT.
YOU'RE SUCCESSFUL WHEN YOUR BROTHER-IN-LAW
     ADMITS IT!
A CHILD IS UNEASY WITH NO LIMITS OF DISCIPLINE.
THE BEST GIFT A FATHER CAN GIVE HIS CHILDREN IS TO
     LOVE THEIR MOTHER.
DISCIPLINE OUT OF CONTROL IS ABUSE.
ABUSE OF WIFE AND CHILD PROVES NOT STRONG BUT
     WILD.
REPORT CHILD ABUSE BEFORE IT'S TOO LATE.
CHURCH FRIENDS PREVENT PARENTAL FIENDS.
DON'T PASS ON CHILD ABUSE.
LOVE YOUR MATE AND STOP DEBATE.
DON'T PASS ON AN UNHAPPY CHILDHOOD. GOD CARES.

YOU

TO MAKE THIS WORLD BETTER, IMPROVE YOURSELF.
GIVE GOD FREEDOM WITH YOUR PLANS TODAY.
YOU GET WHAT YOU SPEAK.
TO POSSESS MORE THAN YOU NEED MAKES YOU CARE-
WORN!
YOUR WORK IS A PORTRAIT OF YOURSELF.
GOD COULD USE YOUR TONGUE!
GOD WILL BRING GOOD FROM ALL, IF YOU ALLOW HIM!
YOU ARE KNOWN BY THE SILENCE YOU KEEP!
RUNNING FROM YOURSELF LEAVES YOU EXHAUSTED!
GOD WANTS TO HEAR FROM YOU TODAY!
THERE'S LITTLE MARKET FOR YOUR TROUBLES!
THE FORCE OF THE UNIVERSE WANTS TO WORK IN YOU!
YOU CAN BREAK SELF ON GOD'S SPIRITUAL LAWS!
YOU CANNOT GO WHERE GOD IS NOT!
TELL THE WORLD WHAT YOU'RE FOR!
LIVING AS THOUGH YOU HAD A MILLION YEARS?
COMMIT ALL YOU DO TO GOD.
YOUR LIVER REACTS TO YOUR STATE OF MIND.
GOD NEVER FORGETS WHO YOU ARE!
GOD IS IN YOU FOR GOOD!
"FEET OF CLAY" DON'T HAVE TO WIPE YOU OUT!
NOT TO INSULT YOU, BUT THERE'S A HIGHER INTELLIGENCE
THAN YOURS!
DEVELOP AN EAR TO WHAT YOU'RE SAYING TO YOURSELF!
YOUR GOD IS READY TO FORGIVE THE PENITENT.
SAY — GOD KNOWS YOU BY NAME!
DO UNTO OTHERS AS GOD DOES TO YOU!
OF ALL YOU WEAR, YOUR EXPRESSION IS MOST IMPORTANT!
EASIER TO DO IT RIGHT THAN EXPLAIN WHY YOU DID IT
WRONG!
FOCUS ON YOUR PAIN AND IT'LL GET WORSE!
WHEN YOU KNOW GOD LOVES YOU, YOU CAN BE TRULY
HONEST.
GOD MAY NEED YOU TO HELP IT HAPPEN.
GIVE OF YOUR BEST TO THE MASTER.
THE WORLD HAS NEED FOR YOU!

WITH GOD YOU'RE NOT THE ONE KEEPING SCORE.
THERE IS A GOD-SHAPED PLAN FOR YOUR LIFE.
GOD WILL NOT FORCE HIS WAY ON YOU.
GOD NEVER FORGETS YOU.
YOU DON'T HAVE TO TRY EVERYTHING BEFORE GOD.
YOU ARE THE TADPOLE OF AN ANGEL.
YOU MAY SAVE A LIFE BY CARING FOR SOMEONE.
DON'T FEED YOUR CONSCIENCE SOFT LIES!
A SMILE WILL MAKE YOU FULLY-DRESSED!
WHATEVER YOUR PAST, YOU HAVE A SPOTLESS FUTURE!
YOU CAN IMPROVISE AN ALTAR AT YOUR BEDSIDE!
GOD WANTS YOU AS A LIVING SACRIFICE.
YOU CAN HANDLE TEMPTATION WITHOUT YIELDING TO IT.
TO GOD YOU ARE IMPORTANT.
GOD IS INVOLVED AND WANTS YOU TO BE.
UNLESS YOU TRY MORE THAN YOU CAN DO, YOU'LL NEVER
    DO ALL YOU CAN!
YOUR SMILE IS SOMEONE'S NECESSITY TODAY!
GOD CAN BE YOUR LIGHT AND YOUR SALVATION.
WHERE YOU ARE RIGHT NOW IS HOLY GROUND.
YOU CAN'T BE WRONG WITH MAN AND RIGHT WITH GOD.
COUNT ON GOD TO DIRECT YOU!
THAT WHICH YOU FEAR MAY WELL COME UPON YOU.
YOU CAN TELL A NATION'S IDEALS BY ITS ADS.
IF LONELY ASK, "WHO BUILT THE WALLS?"
YOU DON'T HAVE TO EARN GOD'S LOVE.
EVEN IF YOU DON'T LOVE YOURSELF, GOD LOVES YOU.
WHAT YOU KEEP THINKING MAKES YOU WHAT YOU ARE.
GOD KNOWS ALL YOUR WAYS, YET LOVES YOU!
YOU DON'T DRIFT INTO THE KINGDOM OF GOD!
YOU DON'T HAVE A CORNER ON A TOUGH LIFE!
DON'T GO TO BED ON YOUR ANGER!
GOD IS YOUR REFUGE AND STRENGTH!
IN SELF-RIGHTEOUSNESS, YOU ALWAYS WIN!
THOU SHALT KEEP THE SABBATH HOLY!
IF YOU'RE NOT LIVING IT, YOU DON'T HAVE IT!
IF YOU ASK, HE RESPONDS, "BE CLEAN!"
YOU DON'T HAVE TO PARK BRAINS TO LOVE GOD WITH
    MIND.
YOU'RE MORE THAN YOUR BEST UNDERSTANDING OF SELF!

SAY — YOU'RE NOT THE ONE KEEPING SCORE!
YOUR BODY IS THE TEMPLE OF THE SPIRIT.
LET THE LORD BE YOUR SHEPHERD AND YOU'LL NOT WANT.
IF YOU WANT REAL TRUTH, GO TO THE SOURCE.
LET HIS PERFECT LOVE CAST OUT YOUR FEAR!
THOU SHALT NOT COVET!
YOU CAN'T GET CAUGHT IN PLACES YOU DON'T GO.
GOD IS CRAFTING YOU FOR ETERNITY.
YOU ARE TO LOVE GOD AS YOUR NEIGHBOR AND AS SELF.
GOD WANTS NOT MONEY OR TIME — BUT WILL, FIRST!
GIVE YOUR CLOSET SKELETONS A DECENT BURIAL.
YOU COULD BE TO BLAME FOR YOUR LONELINESS!
DON'T LET A CHILDHOOD FAULT BURDEN YOUR LIFE!
YOU BELONG TO THE POWER YOU OBEY.
YOU'RE NOT A NOBODY — YOU'RE A CHILD OF GOD!
STRESS COMES FROM EXPECTING TOO MUCH FROM YOUR-
    SELF.
GOD HELPS YOUR HOPES TO HAPPEN.
DON'T TALK ABOUT YOURSELF — IT WILL BE DONE WHEN
    YOU LEAVE.
THOU SHALT NOT LIE!
YOU CAN TRUST YOUR CREATOR.
YOU ARE GOD'S GOOD IDEA.